HOME DI

HOME DECORATION

John Alexander

PELHAM BOOKS

First published in Great Britain by
PELHAM BOOKS LTD
52 *Bedford Square*
London, W.C.1
1970

7207 0073 6

Set and printed in Great Britain by
Tonbridge Printers Ltd, Peach Hall Works, Tonbridge, Kent,
in Baskerville eleven on twelve point, on paper supplied by
P. F. Bingham Ltd., and bound by
James Burn at Esher, Surrey

CONTENTS

ILLUSTRATIONS

Chapter 1: THE TOOLS YOU NEED

Don't be overawed by the impressive displays of decorating tools that you will see in good class stores; the amateur's basic requirements are few, simple and relatively inexpensive, with the possible exception of brushes.

There are two schools of thought about brushes: One is to buy the best quality you can afford – long bristled affairs, thick and silky to the touch – that will last a lifetime, properly looked after. The other is to buy cheap brushes and be prepared to renew them frequently.

This latter view has probably found favour with a lot of home decorators because they tend to be accident-prone with brushes. They stand them in water or white spirit and forget about them until evaporation leaves behind a sad, stiff stick. Or, the bristles get distorted, paint hardens in the stock and the bristles lose their spring. But brush care is really simple and trouble free, if you follow the advice given later in this chapter, and anyone who has used a good quality brush once will be reluctant to settle for anything less thereafter.

For painting walls and ceilings, a 3 in. brush will be adequate. A tradesman would normally use a 4 in. brush, but his wrist and arm have been toughened by years of practice and you would probably find it unwieldy. For emulsion paint, use a 6 in. distemper brush or roller, and complete your kit of paint brushes with $1\frac{1}{2}$ and 1 in. brushes for doors, skirtings, window frames, etc., and a $\frac{1}{2}$ in. brush for cutting-in around panes of glass and fine mouldings. You will also need a paperhanger's brush, a pasting brush, and perhaps a stiff wire brush for exterior preparation of metal guttering, downspouts and similar materials.

Preparation tools you will find essential are a 3 in. stripping knife, a putty knife and some form of scraper. The stripping knife will be used to remove old paint and wallpaper, and for filling large cracks in plaster and wood. The putty knife, apart from helping you to make a neat job of re-glazing a window, is also a useful mini-trowel for filling small cracks, mixing fillers, and as a small scraper. For scraping wooden mouldings around window frames, the flat edges of narrow glazing bars and similar applications, you can use either a shavehook or a proprietary scraper. A shavehook has either a triangular blade, or a blade shaped in a series of curves and flats so that it can be adjusted to virtually any surface. Best known of the proprietary scrapers is the Skarsten range. There are several models with shaped interchangeable blades that can be re-sharpened.

A stepladder is another essential, and if you haven't one already, choose a model with a hinged platform at the top, so that you have somewhere to stand cans of paint and tools. Use it in conjunction with a sturdy plank and a stout box such as a beer crate, and you will be spared the time-wasting effort of climbing up and down the steps to move them along to the next point. If you decide to buy a ladder for outside work it must obviously be long enough to reach the highest point of your house – probably a gable. In most cases, a two-section 12 ft. ladder extending to about 20 ft. will take you comfortably to the eaves – the point where the walls meet the roof – but check before buying that it is long enough to reach any gable end.

A reputable brand-name is your best guarantee of a sound ladder. It will have rectangular hardwood rungs reinforced by a galvanised metal tie-rod underneath each rung. Some of the more expensive models, have metal alloy rungs and wooden stiles. In or near most big towns, there are also plant hire firms that will rent a suitable ladder by the day or week.

The only other essential equipment you will need is a selection of containers – a bucket, a few jars of varying sizes, a couple of 2 pint paint kettles and an S-hook. The communal kitchen bucket can be used for preliminary washing down, but you ought to have your own for the 'clean' jobs, such as rinsing, mixing paste, etc. The jars will be needed for cleaning brushes, and paint kettles for holding paint. Using paint straight from the can causes a build-up of dried paint on the rim and sides of the can, which can flake off into the paint and thus be transferred to your brush. Also, you might need a kettle for outside painting because paint tins do not always have handles. Plastic paint kettles are the cheapest and the best because they are easier to clean than the galvanised metal type. Non-drip paints, however, should always be used direct from the can.

There are many other useful tools that will make life a lot easier for you, and an electric drill comes at the top of the list. With sanding attachments and wire brushes, you can effortlessly prepare old surfaces in a fraction of the time it would take by hand. A paint stirring attachment relieves you of the wrist-racking action of mixing the pigment – and perhaps skimping the job. And, of course, these are only a few of the uses an energetic handyman would find for his drill.

A blowlamp takes all the hard work out of stripping old paint and is less costly in the long term than chemical paint strippers. There are paraffin and methylated spirit lamps that are economical to buy and to use, and bottled-gas burners that are fixed to throw-away gas cartridges. Methylated spirit lamps, however, are not powerful enough for exterior work. Gas cartridges are ideal for small jobs, but would be a rather expensive way to burn off, say, the house exterior. Efficient electrically heated burners are also available, but these lack the mobility of the other types.

A decorator's pasting table for paper hanging is easier to work on than the kitchen table or floor, and while it isn't necessary to own paper-hanger's scissors, a long-bladed pair with rounded ends will make easier the job of trimming lengths of paper.

There are a few simple tools that you could make yourself – for example, a plywood tray to hold paint cans and brushes on the top of old-type stepladders that do not have a platform. Screw to one side of the tray a pair of angle brackets so that they will hook under the top tread of the steps. Make your own plumb bob for checking vertical alignment by filing the end of a heavy bolt to a point and tieing a length of string round the head. Make a plasterer's 'hawk' – a hand-held platform – from a square scrap of wood nailed end-on to a short length of broomstick; a hook to hang paint kettles over a ladder rung from aluminium strip bent to an S-shape; a wallpaper pasting board from hardboard sheet nailed to a framework of 2 × 1 in. softwood. Such a board could be slipped over a short kitchen table, if blocks of wood were pinned to the underside to coincide with the table edges, so that the board would be prevented from slipping about.

Finally, a word about tool care. Keep them all clean, and, where appropriate, sharp and shiny. When you have finished a filling job with plaster or other similar material, scrape the excess off the hawk and wipe it clean with a wet sponge or rag. Rinse off scrapers and putty knives and dry them at once so that they don't rust. File or glasspaper the edges of scrapers to keep them sharp. Keep paraffin blow lamps clean so soot doesn't block the jet, and disconnect the burner unit from a dispensable gas cartridge when not in use, or the remaining gas might imperceptibly leak away.

And be fastidious to the point of neurosis with your paint brushes! Most amateurs remove enamel paints from them with white spirit and tend to be mean with it, because it's an expensive commodity. So take a tip from the tradesman and use paraffin – it's just as effective and cheap enough to encourage you to be generous. Follow this simple drill to keep your brushes clean and supple: First, remove as much excess paint as you can from the brush by drawing it across the side of the paint kettle. Then using the back of an old knife, scrape the bristles from stock to tip and when you can no longer extract paint, wipe them on sheets of newspaper. You can now work the bristles in a bath of paraffin deep enough to cover the brush stock, to loosen the paint that has reached the bristle roots. Press the brush down, so that the bristles flare out like a skirt. After a few minutes of this, shake the excess paraffin out of the brush (the bottom of the garden is a good place to go) and repeat the process with about half as much paraffin. After a further shake-out, try pressing the brush into a small amount of paraffin in a shallow dish. If you have been thorough enough so far, the liquid should have the merest tinge of colour and when this stage is reached, the brush can be washed out in a solution of a mild household detergent, then rinsed until the water runs clear. Shake out the excess moisture, smooth the bristles into their original chisel shape and hang the brush up to dry. A good quality brush will have a hole in the handle for the purpose; if yours hasn't, make one. Brushes put away while damp in a drawer or airless cupboard may become mildewed.

This cleaning technique also applies to brushes used for varnish and cellulose paints, but here the solvents will be methylated spirits and cellulose thinners respectively. Emulsion and acrylic paints are removed by water.

Never leave brushes standing in water because it will eventually cause the ferrules to rust, thus weakening the setting of the bristles and perhaps causing rust flakes to get mixed up with, the paint. When leaving brushes in solvent for a few hours suspend them up to the stock in the liquid with the bristles clear of the container's bottom. Simply standing them in a jar will, in time, distort the bristles. If you accidentally allow paint to harden in a brush, treat it with a brush restorer, such as Dulite brush renovator, following carefully the instructions on the pack. But be resigned to an inferior brush thereafter, because the bristles will have lost most of their spring and life.

Frequently throughout this book you will find reference to rubbing down operations using abrasive papers, so let's start with a clear idea of what's what. Sandpaper is a misnomer for abrasive papers made from tiny particles of glass, though 'sanding' is accepted as both an adjective and a verb. The two kinds of abrasive paper you will find most use for are glasspaper and silicone-carbide paper, better-known as 'wet-or-dry' because it can be used wet or as it comes. Silicone-carbides are the best, but too expensive for general use; glasspaper, on the other hand, clogs readily, whereas a wet silicone-carbide paper won't hold the paint it is stripping. Glasspaper loses its cutting power when damp, so always keep it in a dry place.

The following are the various grades you will be using. There are many others, but these should be sufficient to cover domestic needs.

M2 glasspaper for really coarse work, such as shifting stubborn paint flakes on a stripped surface.

No. 1 or No. 0 for new wood to be painted and as a follow-up to rubbing down with M2.

180 silicone-carbide paper for rubbing down an undercoat ready for the top coat, and rubbing down old gloss before repainting.

240 silicone-carbide paper for a light rub down between top coats.

280 silicone-carbide paper for wood to be varnished.

Chapter 2: GETTING READY

The saying that decoration is nine-tenths preparation will not be unfamiliar to you, and this gloomy observation is inescapably true. Slipshod beginnings tend to snowball into messy and unsatisfying results. If you need convincing, look around you in your own house, or someone else's. You are likely to find bubbles in paintwork where adhesion has been ruined by damp or grease or dirt; patches and cracks on ceilings and walls showing through new paint because, when the old flaking stuff was scraped off, the bared area wasn't filled; dirt collecting on the paintwork of skirting boards, window frames and other timbers because they have never been sanded smooth. More often than not, you can blame the builders in the first place for this last fault. But take heart from the fact that, apart from laying the foundations of a good job, thorough preparation will speed the work, thus reducing the risk of you becoming bored or tired with the job and committing further slapdash sins.

Begin by stripping the room as bare as possible. Remove ornaments, lampshades, carpets, curtains, small items of furniture, etc. If you cannot remove bulky items to another room, pile them in the centre of the room and cover them with dust sheets. It's a good idea to smear the windows with well-diluted white emulsion paint. If you have to work at night, it will increase the efficiency of the artificial light and hide you from the mocking eyes of friends walking the dog to the pub! For night work, fit a 150 or 200-watt lamp without a shade. It might not avoid shadows altogether, but its harsh glare will help to show up blemishes or patches that the paint brush has missed.

This is the stage at which to check the fabric of the room: Loose floorboards should be renailed, proud nail heads hammered back in place. Doors and windows that are binding on their frames should be planed so that they close easily, allowing about $\frac{1}{8}$ in. clearance for subsequent repainting. Stiff hinges should be scraped free from encrustations of paint and treated with a few drops of light oil, but be sure to wipe off the excess with a rag soaked in white spirit before repainting.

If there is a picture rail you want to remove, do it at this point. It will usually be fixed with nails driven into wooden wall plugs or directly through the plaster into the brickwork and the quickest way to remove it is to prise it away from the wall carefully with an old screwdriver or chisel. However, with this method you will inevitably bring down chunks of plaster with the picture rail and these will have to be patched. An alternative method is to find where the nails are and drive them with a punch through the picture rail, back into the wall. This way, you will be left with quite small holes to make good.

PREPARING CEILINGS

Now you are ready to prepare for redecorating, and the obvious place to start is the ceiling, which must first be washed thoroughly. Try a corner first. Though, you are unlikely to find that ceiling white, or soft distemper has been used these days, you will know quickly if it has because it will come off on the sponge or cloth. Such a ceiling treatment can be removed completely by first soaking it with warm water until soft, then scrubbing it loose with an old brush and rinsing it clear with a sponge and clean water.

The other likely coverings are washable distemper, emulsion, or gloss or eggshell oil paints. Brush off loose dust first, then wash thoroughly with a solution of household detergent or proprietary paint cleaner according to the instructions on the pack. Rinse clean and try not to use a lot of water on the ceiling, though the water in the bucket should be changed frequently. In both cleaning and rinsing, work in thin strips within comfortable arm's reach.

While washing off, be on the lookout for areas where the paint appears loose or otherwise unsound. Flaking paint must be removed and suspect areas tested. Use a scraper, keeping it at an acute angle so the blade does not dig into the plaster, and work out forcefully from the flaking edges until the paint is really stubborn. Feather down the edges of the sound paint so that thcy will merge with the existing surface when fresh paint is applied, and rub down the newly exposed plaster and the whole surface of the sound paint with an abrasive.

Either a pumice block or medium grade wet-or-dry paper are suitable, both being easily obtainable from ironmongers or decorators' shops. Work the abrasive in a circular motion over the area being treated, dipping it frequently into water to keep its surface moist. This acts as a lubricant for the abrasive, which, by producing microscopic scratches on the paint surface, provides a 'key' for the new paint. Abrasive paper works best when wrapped around a cork or wooden sanding block; you will find that a standard sheet of paper, when cut into quarters, is made-to-measure for a $4\frac{1}{4} \times 2\frac{1}{2}$ in. block.

CRACK FILLING

Cracks should be raked out with a stripping knife (small cracks with a putty knife) so that they are wedge-shaped, being wider at the back than at the opening. Dust out loose material with an old brush. Cracks and stripped patches should be filled with a cellulose filler, such as Polyfilla and Dulite Supergrip filler, and adhesion of the material will be aided by first coating the area with a pva adhesive (Glue-All, Dufix, etc.) diluted with about 25 per cent water. Apply the filler while the glue is still tacky. A patch filling should be feathered off at the edges with a slightly damp sponge so that it blends in with the existing surface. Fill cracks so that they are slightly proud of the surface and lightly glasspaper flush with the surface when dry.

Of all the surfaces you will have to work on, the ceiling will give you the hardest time, so if crevices and bare patches left by scraped-off paint make it look like a relief map, it might be best to hide it all behind a thick textured ceiling paper.

To redecorate a ceiling that is already papered can be something of a gamble, because the act of washing it down could spoil or loosen the paper. If it is a heavy embossed paper or one that has already been gloss painted, you will probably get away with it, and the Lincrusta-type relief papers found in Victorian houses will be almost as strong as the ceiling itself. Otherwise, play safe and strip the paper.

PREPARING WALLS

Next, the walls: If they are already papered, they should be stripped. Though you could be lucky and get away with hanging new paper on top of old, there's a distinct risk that the moisture in the new paste will break down the adhesion of the old, causing the whole lot to come away from the wall in areas.

Stripping wallpaper is not an arduous job. It should be soaked in water for about 15 minutes, then more water brushed in. After about another 20 minutes, the glue should be soft enough for the paper to come away with little resistance. Ease it away with a scraper, taking care not to dig the blade into the plaster. Inexpensive products such as Dulite wallpaper stripper and Polypeel contain additives that improve the penetration power of water to make the job easier. If you own a compressed air garden sprayer, fill it with water instead of insecticide and use it to spread an even curtain of water on the paper, thus reducing messy splashes on the floor.

Modern vinyl coated washable wallpapers must first be scored thoroughly, so that the water can penetrate through the backing paper to work on the old paste. A wire brush or serrated scraper, lightly applied, will give the water the opening it needs.

Emulsion paint, being water based, may soften the adhesive and lift the paper if you attempt to paint over it. Experience shows that a coat of emulsion paint will sometimes cause the paper to bubble while the paint is wet, then flatten tight against the wall again when dry, but one can never be sure this will happen.

Painted walls must first be washed in a solution of household detergent. Always work from the skirting board upwards to clean off the dirt, using a sponge or cloth, and afterwards rinse off from the ceiling downwards with frequent changes of water. Flaking paint must be removed, cracks and bare patches filled, and the whole surface keyed as already described in preparing a ceiling.

TREATING NEW PLASTER

A word, now, about newly plastered surfaces – and new can mean a year to eighteen months old. Builders usually apply emulsion paint to new plaster because it is sufficiently porous to allow the moisture in the plaster to dry out. As the moisture dries, you sometimes find patches of white powdery efflorescence on the surface and this should be brushed off with a coarse cloth, then the area wiped clean with a damp cloth. The efflorescence could reappear several times, but is nothing to worry about, provided you remove it before redecoration.

Stick to emulsion paint for the first retreatment, or at the most, apply an inexpensive wallpaper. If you try decorating a wall in this condition with an impervious enamel paint, any dampness will build up beneath it and eventually cause the paint to blister and flake.

New plaster being redecorated should be prepared as already described and then sealed to reduce its porosity. A coat of emulsion paint diluted with 25 per cent water is a satisfactory base for emulsion paints, but if the wall is to receive enamel paint, first seal the surface with a primer recommended by the paint manufacturer. Walls that are to be papered can usually be sealed with one or two coats of a proprietary cellulose wallpaper adhesive such as Polycell, which should be allowed to dry before the paper is hung.

PREPARING WOODWORK

Woodwork is prepared with the same requirements in mind – to produce a clean, smooth, surface free from cracks and craters. So first wash it down thoroughly with particular attention to the bases of skirting boards where there could be a build-up of wax polish smeared on during floor polishing. All unsound paint must be scraped free and the edges of scraped patches feathered down with glasspaper. If you are down to the bare wood, coat the area with priming paint. Fill all depressions and cracks with a wood filler till they are slightly proud of the sound surface, then smooth flush with fine grade glasspaper.

If you expose knots in the wood, or you see dark round patches staining through sound paint, this means that resin from a knot in the wood is bleeding through. The paint should be scraped away from it and two thin coats of shellac knotting applied, allowing plenty of time for drying between the two.

Give the same treatment to any knots exposed by scraping and follow with a coat of primer.

In old houses, there will come a moment when, with generations of paint on the woodwork, it will be quicker to start from scratch, stripping off all the paintwork. A blowlamp provides the least laborious and expensive method, but don't use it near window panes for they will crack under heat. On the edges near glass you could use a chemical paint stripper, such as Dulite paint stripper, though you should find that the paint comes away easily under a hand scraper on such narrow strips. Moulded door panels and cornices are best tackled with a chemical stripper. Some need rinsing with water and some with white spirit, so check the instructions on the tin before going on to the final stage of preparation, which is to sand down to remove all flecks of paint, and roughen sound areas of paint work to make a key for the new paint. Always finish off by wiping prepared surfaces with a clean, fluff-free rag soaked in white spirits.

PREPARING METAL WINDOW FRAMES

In most houses where metal window frames have to be prepared, the frames will usually be of galvanised metal and signs of rust in them should be tackled promptly. Use a medium grade waterproof abrasive paper and remove the worst of the rust. Then apply a proprietary rust treatment, such as Kurust, to the patches of bare metal. Do this at once, regardless of when you intend to apply finishing paint, to prevent any dampness causing fresh coatings of rust. Some modern window frames are made from aluminium, which has a high resistance to corrosion, if maintained conscientiously. All that is normally needed indoors is an occasional wipe over with a damp cloth and a coating of household silicone or wax polish. If you have aluminium frames that have been neglected, clean them carefully with a mild domestic abrasive cleaning powder before applying polish – and see that it doesn't happen again!

Chapter 3: CHOOSING AND USING PAINTS

WHAT YOU CAN FIND IN TODAY'S PAINT POTS

Since plastic emulsion – the first of the 'miracle' paints – arrived about 20 years ago, paint technologists have gone on improving their products until today, the home-improving handyman or woman of average dexterity can compete on equal terms with the skilled tradesman and professional interior designer. Strong claims? Well, let's look at them a little closer.

Not many years ago, there were all sorts of priming paints for all sorts of materials, and it was important to choose and use the right one – knowledge that the unskilled could not be expected to possess. For industrial and commercial purposes, special primers are still widely used, but what might be vital on the Forth Bridge is really of no account in the fourth bedroom. So you can use with confidence one of the all-purpose primers, such as Leyland Universal P101 and Brolac All-purpose primer, on wood, metal, plaster, masonry and most other materials you would normally expect to paint.

Dampness is one of the chief causes of an unsuccessful paint job, and a tradesman develops a nose for it. He will be on the watch for condensation, never start outside in parts where the morning dew might linger, and stop before an evening dew can spoil his work. He knows whether wood is dry enough to paint or not, and, unlike the householder taking a week's holiday to do some painting, he is not under the same pressure to get it finished, regardless of the weather. To assist the unskilled, there is a chemical called Stearamin, which, when added to paint, makes it possible to paint even wet surfaces and improves paint adhesion in generally damp or humid conditions. Also available to take the gamble out of this kind of painting is Carsons Winter Gloss, claimed to be dry enough in an hour to resist condensation, fog, dust and similar hazards.

You will probably never be able to compete with the craftsman on speed, but there are several new products that will enable you to complete a job in a fraction of the time it once took. Brolac Speedon undercoat, for example, is touch-dry within an hour, and ready for a top coat in two. Carsons have produced a combined primer and undercoat, thus cutting out one of the operations on a new surface. It can be diluted for use as a primer only, if required. Several leading paint firms, such as ICI Paints Division, now market heavy density emulsion paints to reduce the number of coats needed, and there are many 'one coat' quick drying enamel paints that need no undercoat.

Another recent domestic introduction is polyurethane paint, originally developed to withstand the harsh conditions of industrial plants, and long-used by yachtsmen for painting boat hulls. Polyurethane paints have a great resistance to abrasion, chipping, and chemical spillages of the sort likely to happen in the home. They will also stand up better than conventional enamels to heat and condensation and are therefore ideal for kitchen and bathrooms. The colour range is wide enough to satisfy most conventional preferences, in gloss and eggshell finishes, and they can be bought in that other extremely useful form – as gelled or non-drip paints.

The latest acrylic paints combine the advantages of emulsion and enamel paints. They are as easy to apply as emulsions, they are water soluble, so that brushes and rollers can be cleaned rapidly under a running tap, yet they dry with a durable gloss or semi-gloss surface just like enamels. One criticism is that they give off a smell while drying that a lot of people find pungently unpleasant.

None of this makes you an interior designer, but manufacturers cater for that, too, with the kaleidoscope of colours they produce. No longer do you have to be satisfied with the pallid pastels in plastic emulsion paints. Most High Street paint shops can these days offer vibrant shades which live up to such exotic names as Fireball, Coral Island and Carnaby Tan. The same applies to enamel paints which come in bold and subtle shades once reserved for the trade in what are called architectural ranges. Take a piece of fabric to the paint shop and the chances are a dealer can match it either by tinting a base colour on the spot with the aid of a special machine, or by selling you tubes of pigment that you add yourself to a base paint.

To make colour scheming easier still, manufacturers are taking more trouble with their give-away paint charts. New presentations are continually appearing but three new ones are Hadfield's colour swatch – strips that can be fanned out like a hand of cards to isolate colours; the Robbialac broadsheet which can be folded for colour comparison; the massive ICI book of full decoration schemes that can be consulted at the paint shop.

For further advice on interior decoration, see Chapter 8.

Though not strictly paint, there is another new decorative finish worth mentioning here, and that is the polyurethane stain. Clear polyurethanes have become well established as the handyman's handy substitute for conventional varnishes and french polishes. Coloured polyurethane stains are just as easy to apply. They are for use on bare wood and will colour the surface without obscuring the grain. Again, the colours are rich tones of red, turquoise, gold and so on and more details of their application are given in Chapter 7.

PAINTING LARGE AREAS

With very little practice, the amateur can quickly get the feel of painting when it's confined to small areas, but he often goes wrong in tackling a large expanse of wall or ceiling – particularly when using enamel paints, which need care in brushing out. But there is a basic technique and sequence in painting that will ensure satisfactory results if it is followed properly. Within limits, the secret of success lies in confidence. Full, near-flamboyant strokes will produce better results than hesitant, jerky ones. You will also work faster and enjoy it more.

Dip the brush into the paint so that about a third of the length of the bristles is covered. That way you won't pick up too much or too little paint. Apply the brush to the wall and draw it down in a stripe until it begins to run out of paint. Don't lay on heavily. Recharge the brush with paint and make a similar stripe about a brush-width away and continue like this until you have covered about a yard's width of wall with stripes.

Then without picking up any more paint, join the stripes with a series of backward and forward horizontal strokes until the paint is spread evenly over the area, but leaving the open edges ragged. (See Fig. 1.) Finally, make a series of light strokes vertically to lay off the paint in one direction.

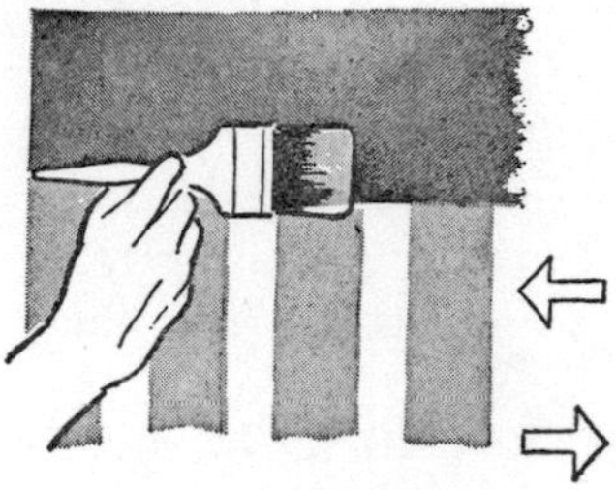

Fig. 1. Painting a wall

Move along and repeat the process on the next yard of wall, and when you come to the horizontal brushing-in, work the strokes well into the ragged edge of the previous patch, so that the two will merge. Leave hard open edges to each patch and there is bound to be a build-up of paint that could show when dry.

Continue across the wall in this way and when the first row is complete, start again immediately under the first section to be painted. This time, work the vertical strokes well into the section above. The laying-off strokes should be made from bottom to top, lifting the brush like a plane taking off, just within the previously painted section.

The technique of painting up to a ceiling, wall junction or other surface that you don't want to touch is called cutting-in and is best done with a 1 in. brush. When painting a wall, these junctions should be done first. Load the brush with paint as already described and, turning it edge-on, place it on the wall about ½ in. away from the line you are working to. Gently apply sufficient pressure to spread the bristles into the angle and draw the brush along in a continuous stroke, maintaining the same pressure and keeping your eye on the line. With a little practice, you should achieve a tolerably clean line, and it's a less tedious method than using masking tape. Incidentally, never use cellulose tape as a substitute for decorators' paper masking tape – it will probably pull off patches of paint when you remove it.

Ceilings are tiresome things to paint, and if you have never tackled a big area before, practise on a wall first, if possible. But of course, the ceiling should be treated first in a total redecoration scheme, and you will save a lot of energy if you can work from a plank instead of hauling a step ladder about.

The trick is not to overstretch yourself. Work in narrow strips about 12 to 18 in. wide within a comfortable arm's reach in both directions. Start at the opposite end from the room's main source of light and work across the ceiling towards the main window.

Paint a long wall by working in vertical strips about 2 ft. wide from ceiling to skirting board. Start on the right hand side if right handed and the opposite end if left handed. On a narrow wall, work in horizontal strips from the ceiling downwards, always remembering to leave the open edges of each newly-painted area ragged for merging with the next.

The brushing out action must not be overdone where thixatropic, (non-drip) paints are being used. Being of a thick, gelled consistency, they can and should be applied generously without risk of curtaining.

Sometimes, it seems hard work to apply enamel paints, but the temptation to thin them should be resisted because overthinning will dull the gloss. A fresh can of paint should not be thinned, but on re-opening a half-full can that has been standing a long time, you may find that some evaporation of the solvents has occurred particularly with polyurethane paints – and then a little thinners will be needed to restore an easy flow to the paint. Add the thinners a few drops at a time and stir in thoroughly.

ROLLER PAINTING

The technique of painting with a roller is slightly different. First, cut-in the edges that the roller cannot reach with a small brush and after applying stripes of paint, as with a brush, spread the paint evenly over the area by rolling it in all directions. To avoid overloading the roller with paint, immerse no more than about a 1 in. section of the roller in the paint, then work it freely back and forth in the dry section of the tray until the pile is fully covered.

When you come to painting the woodwork, follow this sequence: 1. The door, closed first and then wedged open to do the edges; 2. The door frame; 3. Window frames; 4. Picture rail, if any; 5. Skirting board. Before tackling the skirting board, go over the adjacent floor gently with a damp cloth to lay any dust that may have accumulated since you started work.

PAINTING DOORS

Flush doors present no problem, being no more than a miniature wall, but there is a definite sequence to follow when painting a panelled door. Using a small brush, do the mouldings first, then the panels, then the centre vertical rail, the horizontal rails, and finally the outer vertical rails and their edges, as necessary. The rule with edges is that they should be the colour of the side from which they are seen. Thus, when repainting a bedroom, you would paint the opening edge of the door, but leave the hinged edge the colour of the landing woodwork.

The text books usually say one should remove door handles, bolts, etc., but it is a counsel of perfection that can generally be ignored. Knobs and escutcheons can be painted round; lever handles can get in the way but it takes only a modicum of care to avoid patchy or runny workmanship. More important is the finish at a door edge where there is a change in colour. To reduce overlapping smears, apply the paint up to the edge with horizontal strokes, then lay-off vertically. If there are any smears over the edge, remove them at once with a clean rag moistened with the appropriate paint solvent.

PAINTING WINDOWS

Paint the hinged edges of casement windows the interior colour and leave opening edges the colour of the exterior.

Window frame painting should start with a small brush at the edge nearest the glass. Where the panes are small, paint all the glazing bars before treating the main frames – top member

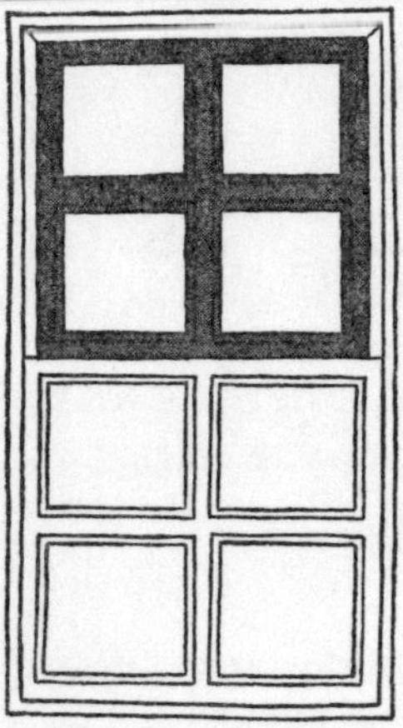

Fig. 2a. First stage in painting a sliding sash window

Fig. 2b Second stage in painting a sliding sash window

first, then the sides and bottom, working outwards from the mouldings on to the flat faces.

When painting sliding sash windows you will avoid getting into a mess if you follow this system: Starting with the window closed, paint the upper (outer) sliding sash as far as you can and the inside of the box frame in which it slides. (See Fig. 2a.) Be careful to apply paint sparingly to the inside of the box frame; too thick a coat in the sliding channel could result in jamming when the windows are opened. Next, open the outer sash slightly to complete painting its top bar, then push the inner (bottom) sash to the top so that you can paint the bottom frame of the outer sash (See Fig. 2b.). At this stage paint the bottom half of the box frame. Now drop the inner sash so that you can paint its top and bottom edges and complete the box and frame – glazing bars first, then frame mouldings, and finally the flat faces of the frame, as for other types of window.

Two further points about painting any kind of window – avoid a thick build-up of paint on frame mouldings and decide at the outset to paint 'free hand' without getting smears on the glass. Many amateurs cheerfully allow the brush to run over on to the pane, removing the surplus when dry with a razor blade. There's nothing wrong with this, but a window pane is the ideal place to perfect your cutting-in technique for places where you cannot clean up afterwards with a razor blade.

Metal frames need regular maintenance if corrosion is to be kept at bay and special attention if it has broken through. And it will, even on galvanised frames, if they are neglected. The paint must be removed completely where rust shows through so that you can treat the frame against further attack. Use a proprietary chemical paint stripper or a scraper to expose the affected parts and cover them at once with Kurust, Galvafroid or other anti-rust agent.

USING A SPRAY GUN

For the average householder, the advantages of painting with a spray gun are arguable. It is true that less physical effort is needed, and that spraying is quicker than brushing. But the energy put into painting is slight in comparison with that expended on the preliminary cleaning and sanding down. Also, using a spray gun involves extra preparation in the form of careful masking of those areas not to be treated, so it is hardly worthwhile except for extremely large areas. It is also true that a better finish is possible with a spray gun, correctly used, but the risk of paint runs is greater if you don't handle the gun as you should.

A spray gun is easier to clean than a set of brushes, but paint has to be thinned before it can be used in a gun and the pressure and jet adjustments have got to be just right, and the paint strained to ensure there are no solid particles to block the delicate jet. Blockages and incorrect pressures can cause unsightly splodges that will have to be brushed out and re-sprayed. And, of course, the technique of using a spray gun has to be mastered; hold the gun too close to too long in one spot and runs or drops might spoil the result. Hold it too far away and you will get a thin coat needing respraying.

The gun nozzle should be held about 10 in. from the surface, and it should never be swung across the work in an arc. Work steadily across the surface on a constant parallel track, starting the spray at one end and releasing the trigger to stop it at the other. If you keep the spray going as you move down to the next section, a thick build-up of paint will result at each end. Always spray mouldings and corners first, 'firing' straight at the edge of an external corner to ensure even distribution of paint over the angle.

AEROSOL SPRAY PAINTS

There are certain small, fiddly jobs which cry out for the use of a spray gun such as painting walls behind radiators and the ornate plaster mouldings found in many older houses.

Obviously, it is not worth buying such an expensive tool for such limited applications, but there are two products that will overcome these difficulties inexpensively. One is the throw-away aerosol paint sprayer, if you find a colour that matches or complements the rest of the scheme. The other is the Humbrol Jet-Pak, a unit in which you can use your own paint. It comprises an aerosol propellant cartridge and a paint container with a spray nozzle. You simply fill the container, connect the aerosol can and fire away.

For about 6s., you can master the technique of handling paint in aerosol cans by refurbishing, say, an old table lamp base, or a kitchen chair. To contain the paint mist, enclose the article – if it's small, in a grocer's delivery carton; if it's large, in a clothes horse draped with newspapers. The instructions on the aerosol can say 'shake for 30 seconds after the agitator rattles' and from time to time during spraying operations. Ignore this and your work will most likely be spoiled with a splutter of thick pigment. It's a good idea to store aerosol cans on their sides to keep the pigment partially mixed. When you shake the can, you should eventually feel the liquid inside moving about, a sign that it is thoroughly mixed. Hold the can about 12 in. from the work and spray in short, sharp bursts, particularly at crevices where the paint will quickly build up and run. A great advantage with aerosol paints is that they dry in about seven minutes.

PAINTING RADIATORS

For some obscure reason, radiators often used to be painted with a metallic paint, and if you are thinking of treating yours to a coat of gleaming gold, bronze or silver – don't. Metallic paints are reflective, and will cause the interior heat of a radiator to 'bounce' back on itself. The result can be a reduction of up to 15 per cent in the total heat output of a radiator, and up to a 50 per cent reduction in the direct radiated heat, that is the heat you personally feel coming from the radiator, as distinct from the output which goes into warming the air.

Another thing to avoid is an undue build-up of coats of paint, for these will have something like the same effect. You can prevent an excessively thick paint film by giving a radiator a thorough rub-down with abrasive paper each time you repaint. Don't in a fit of enthusiasm, decide to use a power tool and sanding disc to remove the old paint. In doing so, you could also remove some of the welding at the seams, leading to eventual weakening and leakage.

Just as there is a long-held convention that radiators should be treated with metallic paints, there is another that says one should never paint them a dark colour, and this is equally mistaken. There is no reason why dark colours should reduce a radiator's efficiency.

When calculating how much paint you are going to need for a particular job, err on the credit side where there is an element of doubt. Most makers stipulate that they cannot guarantee an exact match of a shade from batch to batch, so there could be a minute difference if you have to order an additional can later and, anyway, you wouldn't want to run out of paint in the middle of a room. The following table provides a practical working guide to the coverage from one pint of paint on smooth surfaces at the rate of one coat.

Emulsion paint 90 sq. ft.
Gloss paint 100 sq. ft.
Undercoat 80 sq. ft.
Priming paints 60 sq. ft.

Chapter 4: TYPES OF WALLPAPER AND HOW TO HANG THEM

For pattern and texture, there has never been anything to beat wallpaper at the price, and the recent development of vinyl coated wallpapers has produced a perfectly acceptable treatment for bathroom, kitchen and nursery walls where they will have to withstand harsh treatment from steam, grease, grubby fingers, etc. Because they are non-porous, vinyl papers must be hung with special adhesives, such as ICI's Dulite Vinyl Adhesive, that contain ingredients to prevent mould growth in the plaster. Your wallpaper shop will supply a suitable adhesive. Some vinyl papers have a built-in labour saving aid: When the time comes to repaper, you simply ease away a corner of the pattern with a finger nail, and the whole piece will peel off, leaving a backing paper behind as a liner for the new paper. Crown Cleenstrip and ICI's Vymura are two examples.

All except the cheapest wallpapers are usually classified now as spongeable, washable or scrubbable. A spongeable paper can be wiped over with a damp cloth and the colours will not run. A washable paper – generally vinyl coated – can be cleaned with a solution of mild detergent, and its tougher, scrubbable brother will withstand occasional mild scrubbing or the use of household scouring powders to remove stains.

In addition to a wide range of printed patterns, the elegance of traditional flock wallpapers is also reproduced in vinyl, nowadays, as are satin stripe, silk and rough textured effects.

Conventional papers can be hung with cold water paste, but even tradesmen mostly tend to use the modern cellulose pastes, and being non-staining, they are eminently suitable for the inexperienced paper hanger.

Decide first whether a lining paper is necessary. It will be if the walls are in poor condition, and if a heavy paper is to be hung. Choose heavy quality lining paper and hang it horizontally with an overlap at the joints. Seal bare plaster first, whether lining or applying the wallpaper direct. Cellulose pastes can be thinned for this purpose, if you follow the directions on the packet, or a traditional wallpaper size can be purchased.

'DRY' PLANNING

A little preliminary planning is necessary before you start hanging paper. When calculating the amount of wallpaper needed, remember that a standard English roll is 21 in. wide and 11 yds. long. How many wall lengths you will get out of a roll will depend on the size of the pattern, or the 'repeat' as the man in the shop will call it. With a big pattern there will be more wastage in matching the lengths than with a small one, but it is often possible to reduce this wastage by working with three or four lengths at a time. Cut a trial length, allowing 2 or 3 in. wastage at top and bottom, lay it on the pasting table and use it as a guide for cutting the subsequent lengths the most economical way.

Another preliminary test that's worth doing is to run out a short length of each roll, overlaying them to check that there is no slight difference in colour. It does happen sometimes, and if you know about it, the odd rolls can either be changed or set aside for a wall where the discrepancy will not be noticed.

If the chosen pattern is a big, dominant one, the hanging of the wallpaper must be planned so that the room looks balanced when completed. This means centring the first length on the focal point of the room, which is usually the chimney breast, and working out from there around the room in both directions. If you choose a textured, striped, or small-patterned paper, start in a corner near the main window and work round the room.

A PERFECT START

If the first piece is hung truly vertical, the rest will follow, and since the wall will almost certainly run slightly off, you will need to strike an accurate guide line. A plumb line can be made from a heavy bolt or similar weight tied to a length of chalked string. Hold the string at a point near the ceiling fractionally more than 21 in. away from the corner in which you are starting. When the weight on the other end rests steady, get someone to tighten the string, pull it back like a bow string, and let it snap against the wall. This will transfer an accurate, vertical chalk mark on the wall to which you can hang the first length of paper.

With a sufficient number of lengths ready cut to size, you are ready to start papering. The paste should be mixed to a consistency where it just drips off the brush. Across the paste bucket, tie a length of wire or string to the handle lugs to act as a rest for the brush and provide a means of wiping excess paste from it while pasting.

You will work better from a proper pasting table and folding models can be bought for £2 or £3, or you could make your own from hardboard and timber framing, as suggested. It should be about 6 ft. long and 22 in. wide – just over the width of the paper. To paste a length, push the paper away from you so that one edge is flush with the far edge of the table and apply the paste from the centre of the length to the far edge with a series of herringbone sweeps of the brush. (See Fig. 3.) Then pull the paper flush with the table edge nearest to you and repeat the process. This routine ensures that no paste is daubed on to the paper. Avoid pasting the last couple of inches at the ends of each length, since these are waste and would merely smear paste on the ceiling and skirting board.

Each length will have to be folded before it can be carried to the wall and as it is bound to be longer than the table, folding takes place as you paste. Having pasted the first section as described for about half the length, take the corners and bring the end over in a fold to the centre of the length. (See Fig. 4.) The meeting edges of the paper should be in line and if they are not, slide the paper until they are; it will slip easily when pasted. The fold should be a soft bend, not a crease. With an extra-long piece or a very short table, it might be necessary to double up on this fold before continuing pasting. Slide the folded portion up the table, paste the remainder and fold this in the same way.

The completed length should then be hung over a chair back

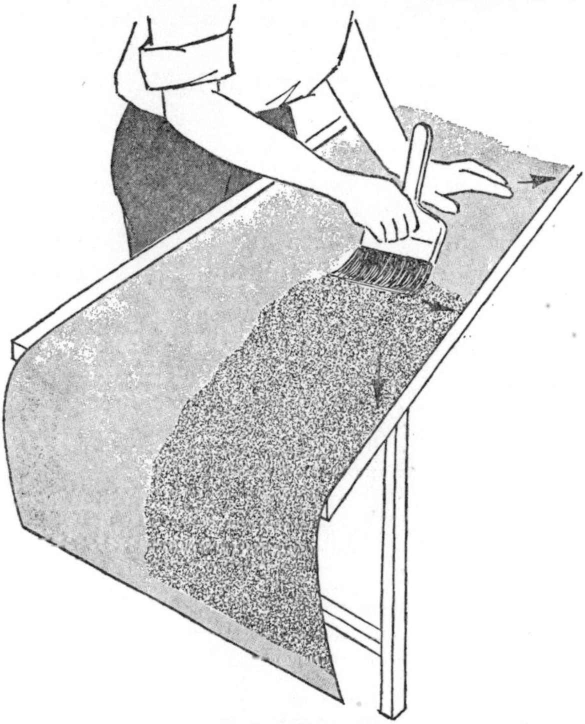

Fig. 3. Pasting wallpaper

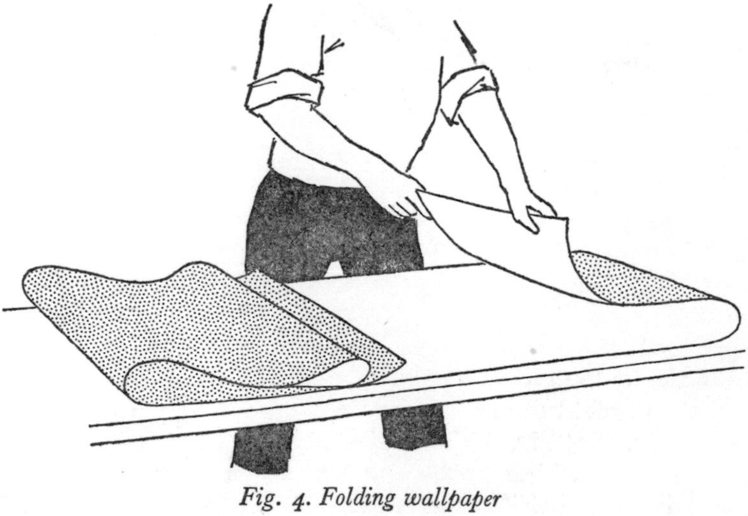

Fig. 4. Folding wallpaper

or other convenient rest and allowed to soak while you get on with pasting one or two more lengths. Depending on its weight, paper should be left to soak before hanging for five to ten minutes. You can tell whether a length is ready by picking it up to see if it hangs limply over your arm.

If you have to make do with the kitchen table for pasting, a slight variation of the method described will help to prevent paste getting on to the pattern. Take the whole stack of cut lengths and place them on the table at least 6 in. back from the edge where you are standing. Draw each length forward for pasting flush with that edge so that the excess paste at the far edge is brushed on to the next length to be treated.

THE RIGHT WAY TO HANG PAPER

Make sure that the ladder is in the right position at the wall and your scissors, brush and a clean cloth are handy before taking the paper to the wall. Drape the folded length over the left arm (if you are right handed) and mount the steps, having checked that in the fold facing you, the pattern is the right way up. Mount the steps and with the right hand peel back the top three inches of the fold. Hold the paper at both corners and allow the first section to unfold, catching the rest of the length as it falls on the instep or knee of the outstretched left leg. (See Fig. 5.) This is to ensure that weight of the falling portion doesn't cause the corners you are holding to tear.

Place the right hand in the centre and near the top of the unfolded portion and press it to the wall, leaving about a 3 in. overlap at ceiling or picture rail. From here, use light pressure from both hands to slide the paper into position against the plumbed line. When satisfied that it registers accurately, run a firm brush stroke down the centre and work the brush down both sides from the centre to press out any air bubbles as the paper is stuck down.

If the first 2 ft. of the length are accurately aligned there is little risk of the rest of the paper running out of true, and you can then unfold the remainder and brush it to the wall in the same way. (See Fig. 6.) The minute you see a wrinkle begin to form when brushing, peel the paper back an inch or two above the point where the wrinkle starts and brush down again.

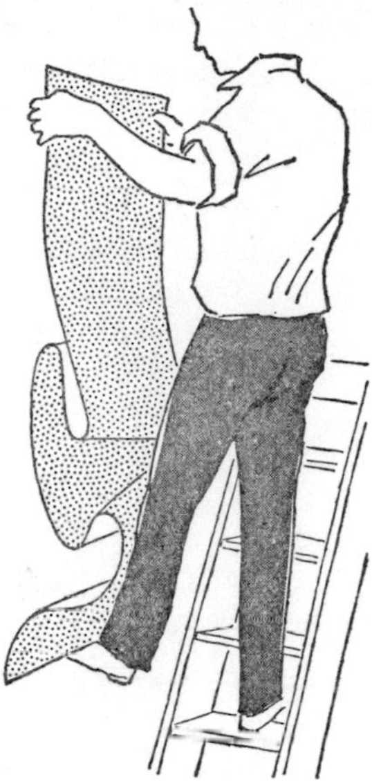

Fig. 5. Hanging a length of wallpaper

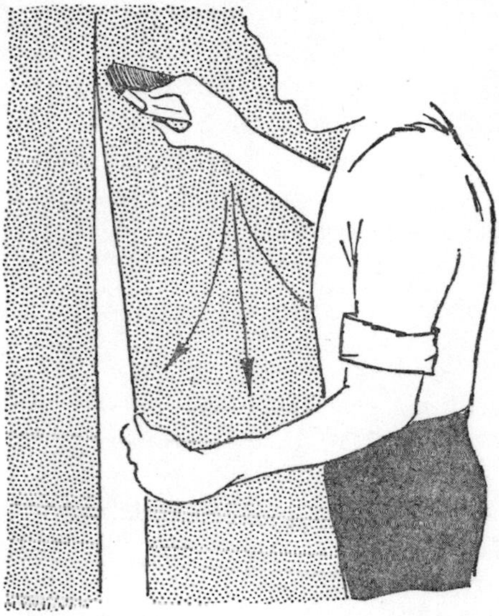

Fig. 6. Brushing wallpaper in place

When the length is hung, run the back edge of the scissors along the top overlap to crease the paper where it is to be cut off. The crease will show on the back of the paper when you peel it from the wall, and you can cut accurately to the mark. Brush the paper in place again and repeat the procedure at the skirting board junction. Subsequent lengths are treated in exactly the same way.

WHEN IT DOESN'T LINE UP . . .

That is the essence of hanging wallpaper, but of course it is never all straightforward, so let us now deal with the snags.

Wallpaper stretches when soaked and will stretch more in patches that have been overpasted. Consequently, you could find in places a tendency for an edge to overlap instead of butt against the adjoining piece or irritating tiny gaps in an otherwise perfect butt joint. Badly trimmed papers will also result in uneven joints, a fault sometimes found in machine-trimmed papers, too. Don't try to re-hang a length in these circumstances because you will only make matters worse. If a joint is really bad, try again with a new length. If the gaps are slight, they can often be closed by stretching the paper with sharp karate chops with the side of the hand. A slight overlap can be 'lost' by stroking the paper down that edge with the brush then dabbing it back to the wall.

WHEN IT BLISTERS . . .

Frequently, blisters appear in the paper after it has been hung without a sign of them. Don't worry. If you have pasted correctly they will disappear as the paper dries. If the odd blister is still there after two or three days, slice the spot with a razor blade as if drawing the spokes of a cartwheel, and carefully sift the pieces so that you can dab the bare patch with a little paste and stick them back.

INTERNAL CORNERS

When turning a length of paper round an internal corner, resign yourself to the fact that the angle won't be vertical and treat it in two parts. If the pattern is discreet, you might get away with cutting the length that turns to allow a 1 in. turn into the angle and overlap it with the next piece. If it's a bold design this treatment would probably produce a distortion and if this cannot be hidden behind curtains, bookshelves or what-have-you, tackle it this way: Paste the wall up to the angle. Offer up an unpasted length of paper and brush it in place to the wall. With the back of the scissors, crease the paper into the angle, peel it away and cut carefully along the outside edge of the crease, lightly repaste and replace. Treat the turn piece in the same way, check with plumb line that it is vertical, then crease and cut so that it neatly butts up against its neighbour.

EXTERNAL CORNERS . . .

On external corners, as found on a chimney breast, the paper should turn the corner at least 2 in. Brush the piece in place up to the turn and nick the surplus top and bottom on the corner. In brushing the overhang round the turn, check that the fixed portion is not dragged away from the joint with its neighbour. To avoid this, you can use the free hand to anchor the fixed portion as you brush. When it's right, crease the surplus, top and bottom, peel back one portion and trim off and rebrush; then do the same with the other. Take your plumb line to the turned edge, and you will probably find that its out of true. The next piece can either be overlapped, or the turned piece trimmed to a true vertical with the aid of the plumb line, so that the next piece can be butted against it.

TRIMMING AROUND A FIREPLACE . . .

If you are papering around a chimney breast, you are probably also papering around a fireplace, which is going to present some awkward cutting in. Smooth the paper down over the mantelshelf, then cut upwards from the bottom of the length approximately to this line, allowing about 2 in. of surplus beyond the overall shelf width, and the same surplus for the lowest point of

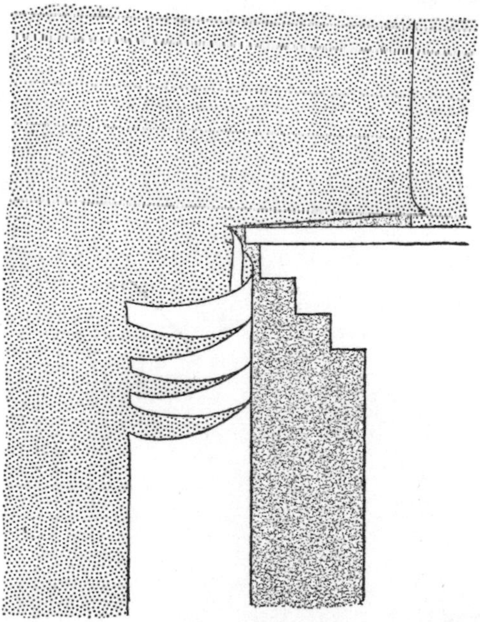

Fig. 7. Trimming in around a fireplace

the fire surround's horizontal projection. From this point, you will have to play it by ear, according to the shape of your fire surround. In most cases it will be virtually impossible to pre-cut the paper exactly to the required shape, and a series of diagonal cuts will be needed to ensure that the paper can be brushed back around the projections. (See Fig. 7.)

. . . AROUND LIGHT SWITCHES

The principle of this will be better understood if we look at another major fiddle you might be involved in – cutting round a circular light switch. To make a neat job here you will have to make a hole in the paper approximately in the centre of the area through which the switch will project and make from this axis a series of spokewheel scissor cuts corresponding roughly with the area of the switch. When brushed back against the wall, the paper will fold naturally around the switch like flower petals and the surplus can then be trimmed off. The same principle applies to flush-mounted square switches, though here the plate can be loosened or removed, and two diagonal cuts are all that are needed in order to tuck the paper behind the plate. (See Fig. 8.) The surplus can then be trimmed off. Always switch the circuit off at the mains before interfering with light switches or flush mounted power sockets.

TRIMMING AROUND DOORS

When papering round a door frame, brush the paper into the angle between the wall and the frame and crease the junction with the back of the scissors. Peel back the paper and cut along the outer edge of the crease mark to the point that corresponds with the top of the door frame, then crease the overhang with the scissors, peel back, cut to the crease mark and brush into place.

TRIMMING AROUND WINDOWS

The trickiest task of all is papering round a window, which, like a fireplace wall, is something of a focal point. A bold pattern should be centred on the window opening but the position may

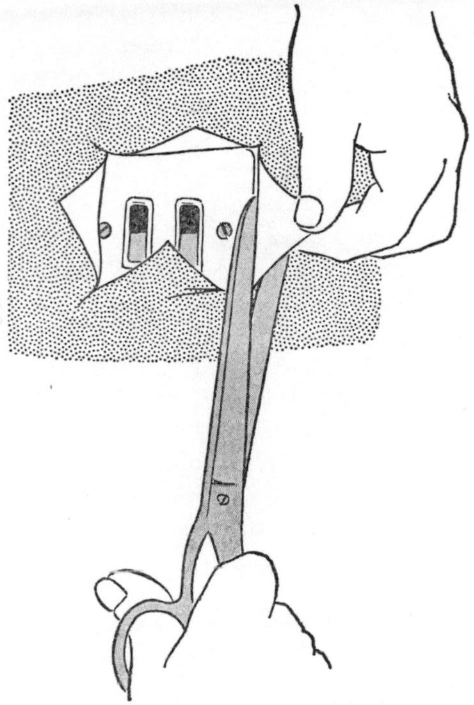

Fig. 8. Cutting in around a light switch

not be critical with a small pattern and with regular stripes you can carry on from the adjacent wall. Taking the most exacting example, start by hanging a bold patterned paper to a lined plumbed centrally above the window, cutting the piece long enough for a turn under the soffit, plus a couple of inches for trimming-in to the window frame. Work outwards in both directions from this point. If the soffit is not true, the pieces turned under could run out of line and if this happens, allow only a ½ in. underlap and cut separate pieces to fill in. At each end of the window, you will be involved in cutting a full length piece to cover part of the wall and to wrap round the window reveal. Work to a plumbed line, allowing for the turn and 2 in. surplus for trimming in around the window frame. Paste in position and run your hand along the paper where it meets the top edge of the soffit. Peel away the paper and cut parallel to about $\frac{1}{2}$ in. outside the crease mark. Similarly crease and cut the paper to fit around the window sill, then brush the paper into the reveal. A small patch will have to be cut to fit the remaining bare corner of the soffit.

PAPERING A HALL . . .

When a hall has to be papered, the amateur is often in a dilemma. He knows he can cope with the bulk of it, but is put off by the long drop in the stairwell, and this is the part that should be done first. We have talked about paper stretching when soaked, and in a stairwell, which will be at least double the normal working length, the stretch could be as much as $1\frac{1}{2}$ in. to which the rest of the paper will have to be matched.

Some sort of scaffold rig is essential for secure and efficient working. Generally, a combination of a step ladder and a section of an extension ladder bridged by a stout plank can be arranged to give access to the high spots. (See Fig. 9.) For

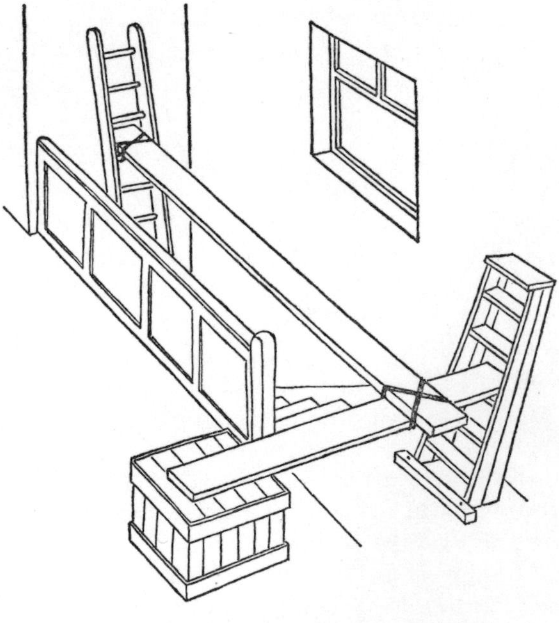

Fig. 9. Scaffolding for a stair well

safety, see that they are lashed firmly together and if possible, have someone standing by to steady a ladder if needs be. You will require help in wrestling with the longest lengths of paper, anyway.

Work to a chalk-mark snapped from a plumb line, as described. In this case it would be more sensible to cut and fit each length of paper as you go. You would also be better off in choosing a simple striped or textured paper, because you could run into difficulty in getting a good match with a large pattern by the time you get to the lower reaches of the hall. The longer lengths should be folded, concertina fashion, in about 18 in. widths to make them easier to handle. At the end of your reach on the scaffold, hand the rest of the folded paper to helper to support until you can get down and carry on. Hang the first section about 1 in. higher – that is cut the usual 3 in. of surplus, but let 4 in. overlap at the ceiling to accommodate the stretch in the paper when you come to match up at the lower level.

When the longest lengths have been hung, complete the bulkhead over the stairs before continuing down, so that the stairs can be cleared of scaffolding. Measure each length for the staircase wall, by creasing it lightly to follow the angle of the staircase skirting and cut parallel with the crease allowing a 3 in. margin for final trimming-in.

PAPERING A CEILING . . .

Gain as much experience as you can of papering walls before attempting a ceiling. Here, it is essential to work from a plank long enough to span the room because you will be handling long pieces of paper and will not be able to stop on the way to readjust your scaffold. A comfortable working height will leave about 6 in. between the ceiling and the top of your head. For best results, stick to a heavy paper or an embossed paper with a small random pattern so that there are no matching problems.

Work should start, if possible, immediately above the main source of light and at right angles to it, but in a long room it will probably be more convenient to work across the light. Start by measuring 21 in. out from the wall in one corner and make a pencil mark at that point on the ceiling. Make a corresponding mark at the opposite end and chalk a length of string that will span the ceiling. You will need someone to hold the other end against the opposite mark, while you snap the string against the ceiling. Use a dark coloured chalk so that the line will stand out against the ceiling.

Cut a length of paper, allowing about 2 in. of waste at each end, and paste it in the manner already described. Ceiling paper needs many more folds than a wall-hung length because of the awkwardness in handling it and because of its greater length, which will probably be 10 ft. or more. Make the folds concertina fashion at about 18 in. widths. The first fold will be paste-to-paste but subsequent folds pattern to pattern.

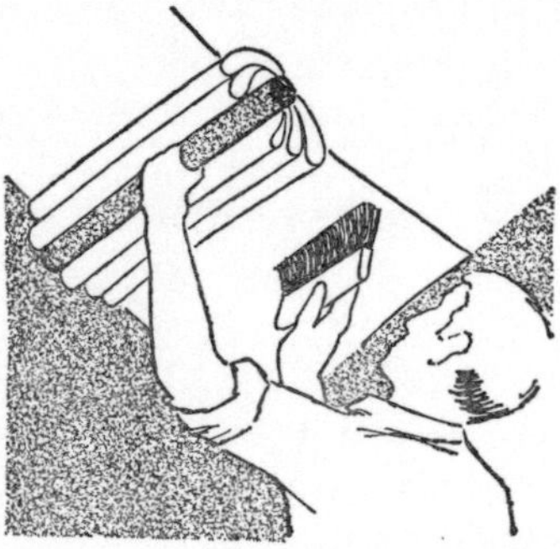

Fig. 10. Applying ceiling paper

Use a spare roll of paper as a support for a folded length when fixing it to the ceiling. On the scaffold, peel open the first fold and support it with the right hand while the left hand supports the rest of the length just clear of the ceiling. Slide the unfolded portion into position on the guide line and brush it out, down the centre and outwards from each side (See Fig. 10.) Now turn and face the direction in which you are going, open the next fold, adjust it to the line and brush down. Continue in this sequence till the length is complete, then mark and cut the waste at each end. Subsequent lengths are butted edge to edge.

Lighting fittings will obviously be taken down, but there's no need to remove a simple ceiling rose and flex. When this obstruction is reached, poke the scissors through the centre of the paper and make a series of star shaped cuts. The paper can then be slipped over the lamp holder and fitted round the rose.

When the paper is dry, it is advisable to give it two coats of emulsion paint which will protect it from the build up of dirt and give you a better surface to clean when the time comes.

Chapter 5: THE CHOICE BEYOND PAINT AND WALLPAPER

For the ambitious home decorator, there's more to creating a scheme worthy of a magazine cover than slapping on paint and wallpaper. Also, these traditional materials are not the best for every situation. A wall may be in such poor condition due to damp or decaying plaster that only resurfacing would produce an acceptable result. The construction of the walls will have some bearing, too, on what you can do with them. Since dampness in one form or another is an ever-present plague in the majority of English homes, we deal with it separately in Chapter 10. Here, let us study the alternatives to paint and paper for wall decoration.

Of increasing popularity in recent years is timber cladding. The best known one is 'knotty pine' or what the timber merchant calls 'deal' and it is the staple wood for housebuilding, from rafters to floor boards. But there are many other forms of timber cladding in such exotic timbers as rosewood, cherry, and black American walnut. These are available only as veneered plywood panels because of the rarity of the woods used, and they can be obtained from most big timber yards, some builders' merchants and do-it-yourself shops.

The standard size is a sheet measuring 8 × 4 ft., though it is possible to get boards 10 ft. long – useful for high rooms in old houses. Generally, the boards are grooved to simulate planking. The grooves can be of random width or regularly spaced, but they are arranged so that there is a groove every 16 in., so that they can be invisibly nailed. A factory applied finish means that they need only an occasional wipe with a damp cloth. A good place to see such boards in situ are modern pubs, banks and places like shoe shops. The technique of fixing them is described later in this chapter. Because these large sheets are somewhat unwieldy to handle, some manufacturers market packs containing three or four boards to make up a width of 4 ft. The long edges of the boards are machined so that they interlock at one of the grooves and there is just enough room to get the nails in. The amateur would find packs easier to work with, especially when trimming into corners.

At upwards of 4s. 6d. sq. ft., these boards are not cheap, and if you would be happy with a more humble wood, the cheapest way to buy timber cladding is in planks from a timber merchant. He will always have knotty pine in stock, and many of the bigger places keep suitable stocks of red cedar. Ask for tongued-and-grooved matching $\frac{3}{8}$ to $\frac{1}{2}$ in. thick; you can get it thicker, but it isn't necessary and it will cost you more. Go to the woodyard when they are not busy and find a timber porter with a friendly face. For the price of a pint, he will more than likely help you sort through the stocks to find boards with lots of knots, which gives the cladding its character. When calculating quantities, you must allow for the tongue and groove in each board. Thus, a 6-in. board will actually cover $5\frac{1}{4}$ in.

New photoprinting techniques have resulted in a range of hardboard claddings with richly simulated veneers that are hardly distinguishable from the genuine veneers on plywood boards. These boards are also grooved to produce a random planked effect and though they are not as durable as the real thing, they are treated with a tough protective finish for a long life, and can be wiped down with a damp cloth to preserve the sheen.

If you live near a big stockist of hardboards, you might be pleasantly surprised by the range of decorative finishes that can be obtained. There are moulded hardboards with fluted, reeded, leathergrain and grass cloth patterns. Plain hardboards can be obtained with hessian and leather-like vinyl finishes in a good range of colours and there are boards with a hard, glossy melamine finish, some of them plain, some of them in a simulated tile finish. Melamine hardboards are ideal for rejuvenating old kitchens, bathrooms and cloakrooms.

Real ceramic tiles have been developed to a point where it is virtually impossible to make a botched job of work. In the old days, the joints between each tile had to be packed with thin card to leave room for grouting paste, but modern tiles have built-in spacer lugs that automatically ensure correct spacing. And tiles are much thinner, so that they are easier to cut and shape.

Cork tiles have long been a familiar sight on floors, but there are now thinner qualities designed for use on walls. The lighter shades look best and there is a specially processed tile called Wicanders Character Walcork that is particularly attractive.

For splashbacks and heatproof worktops in kitchens, there are metal tiles – stainless steel and aluminium anodised to give a copper finish.

Formica, Arborite and the other plastic laminates are widely used commercially as wall claddings because of their terrific resistance to wear. Expense and difficulty of erection rules out their use on large expanses for the householder but they are ideal for splashbacks in kitchens and bathrooms.

Solid vinyls, as distinct from vinyl coated papers, are coming out of the commercial contract field and into the domestic market. In effect, they are similar to wallpapers but are totally impervious to moisture, and, being a great deal thicker, can withstand more cleaning and have an indefinite life. The range of colours is wide and finishes include rough, tweedy, textures, leather grain and watered silk effects. Being so thick, they will often mask uneven patches in a wall which would show through a paper.

Hessian also has this last advantage, as well as being a soft decorative finish. Decorators' hessians are available in a wide range of colours, but they are expensive. Natural upholsterer's hessian, on the other hand, is very cheap and can be emulsion painted any colour you like.

Two other heavy duty wallcoverings that have withstood many a long year of hard wear and changing fashion are Anaglypta and Lincrusta. Both of them are ideal for badly-cracked walls and ceilings, provided the plaster is sound, though you should cut your teeth on simple paperhanging before using them as they are thick and not easy to handle.

Anaglypta comes in heavily sculpted designs in panels simulating the ornate plaster mouldings seen in old houses, and low-relief patterns for hanging like wallpaper. Lincrusta's speciality is realistic simulation of ornate wood panelling in classic forms, though textured patterns are also made. Whereas

Anaglypta is pressed to form its pattern producing hollows on the reverse side, Lincrusta's texture is applied to a flat paper backing. They can both be painted.

Maybe you would like the textured, natural effects that can be achieved with roughly-trowelled plaster and bare brick, as pictured so frequently in glossy magazine features on country properties. The logical way to produce a brick finish is to hack off the plaster, but before you reach for a hatchet, consult a builder, architect or surveyor. Unless yours in an old house – and even if it is – the brickwork beneath the plaster may not provide the attractive, rustic look you expected. Even the expert will not be able to guarantee a rewarding exposure, but he should be able to advise whether it's worth taking a calculated risk or not.

An alternative way of producing a bare brick wall is to cover the existing surface with brick tiles. Though produced basically for exterior wall cladding, there is no reason why they should not be used internally, and they can be ordered from builders' merchants in slate and stone as well as brick colours. However, brick tiles weigh heavily (over half a ton per 100 sq. ft.) and it would be wise to consult a builder before going ahead.

Rough-cast plaster effects can be easily achieved by the amateur, using texture paints – white or pastel-coloured powders to which you just add water and apply with a brush or trowel.

A very attractive and more enduring alternative to plain papering a ceiling is to tile it. Individual tiles would be more manageable than a long length of paper that has to be carefully brushed into place and might not, in the end, totally obliterate imperfections in the plaster. No blemishes will show through ceiling tiles, though of course, the plaster must be in sound condition to support their weight, and you will have discovered whether the plaster is crumbly or not in cleaning the ceiling in preparation for redecorating. An additional advantage with ceiling tiles is that they provide some degree of sound insulation, as they tend to damp down the noise level within a room. They will also help to keep it warmer.

Now let's look in more detail at the techniques involved in using all these materials.

FIXING PLANKS

First a groundwork of 2 × 1 in. timber battens must be fixed to the wall. For tongued and grooved planking, a horizontal batten at ceiling level, another in the centre of the wall and a packing strip to bring the skirting board up to the correct thickness will be sufficient for an 8 ft. high room. For a higher room another intermediate batten might be necessary.

Securely fix the battens with either 2 in. masonry nails, or screws in wallplugs which must penetrate about 1 in. of brick-work beneath any plaster. Fix the battens at about 2 ft. intervals and do not try to force them to follow any uneveness in the wall; gaps between battens and wall should be packed with scraps of hardboard. The methods of achieving wall fixings are described in Chapter 11.

Stack tongued and grooved boards flat on the floor in the room for a few days before laying, so that their moisture content can adjust to that of the room. If they are damp and then dry out in a warm room when erected, they could shrink badly. Floor and ceiling will not be exactly parallel, so if the boards are cut to the same length there will be gaps in places. These can be hidden behind a length of moulding pinned across the boards when they are up, so decide at this stage whether you want the moulding at ceiling or floor level. The alternative is to cut each board exactly to size.

Start in the left hand corner and place a board against the wall with its tongue towards you. Mark on it in pencil the point where it butts against the skirting board on the return wall and cut out a step the thickness of the skirting. You will be accus-tomed by now to find that no wall is truly vertical, so offer up the board again to see how it relates to the wall, now that it is sitting over the skirting. A bad gap between an upright board and sloping wall can either be hidden later with another strip of moulding, or the board can be scribed and cut to follow the line of the wall. To do this, take a block of wood slightly thicker than the widest point of the gap. With the board hard against the return wall and the battens and the block pressed tightly into the angle, draw the block down from ceiling to floor, holding a pencil against the block and the board. You will thus transfer to the board a line that follows the plane of the wall and any marked hollows in it. By sawing carefully to that line, you will produce a snug fit between the board and the wall. Adjust the step for the skirting board, if necessary.

Fix the board to the battens with $\frac{3}{4}$ in. panel pins, driving them at an angle through the tongue. (See Fig. 11a.) The final

Fig. 11a. 'Secret nailing' through tongued and grooved boards

$\frac{1}{8}$ in. of each panel pin will have to be driven home with a nail punch. Swing the hammer in short, sharp blows to avoid hitting the board and bruising it. Take care that the punch doesn't slip or overdrive the panel pin, causing the tongue to split.

Slide the groove of the next board over the tongue of the fixed board and hammer it tightly in position, using a scrap length of 2 × 1 in. batten to protect the tongue. Nail through the tongue as before, and continue across the wall to the last few inches. (See Fig. 11b.)

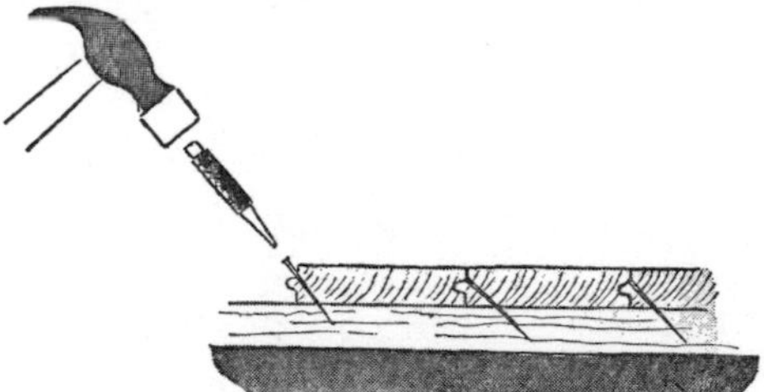

Fig. 11b. Punching the nail heads flush

The last board to be fixed should be scribed in as the first or covered with moulding, but either way you are unlikely to end up with exactly one board to fill the gap. In these circumstances, it's best to fix the last board and any part of another board as one. Cut the final portion to fit and glue and pin it to the penultimate complete board. The panel pins will have to be punched below the surface of the board and the heads filled with a matching wood stopper. Ease the groove over the last exposed tongue and pin the end piece to the battens, again punching and stopping the heads.

The whole surface should now be rubbed down with fine glasspaper in the direction of the grain and given three or four coats of polyurethane varnish.

FIXING DECORATIVE WALLBOARDS

Plywood and hardboard sheets should be fixed to 2 × 1 in. wall battens running horizontally at roughly 2 ft. intervals and to vertical battens centred at 16 in. intervals. Secure the battens as described. All edges of the board must be supported, so you will have to make frames from battening to support any cut-outs for light switches, power points and so on.

The neatness of the finished fixing will largely be controlled by the accuracy of your measurements and saw cuts. For best results use a fine-toothed saw, cutting into the face side of each sheet, and score through pencilled guide lines with a sharp blade.

The chances of an 8 × 4 ft. board just slotting into place in a room 8 ft. high are remote; a slight slope in the floor or bulge in the ceiling will be sufficient to prevent the board from lying flat against the battens. Therefore, it must be cut slightly undersize, so that it just clears floor and ceiling. Then it can be scribed to follow the line of the ceiling or floor, depending on where you wish the gap to occur. Floor level is probably best, because you could cover the gap with a skirting board matching that around the rest of the room. To scribe the board to the ceiling, place wedges under the edge at floor level checking with spirit level or plumb line that the board – and therefore the grooves – are vertical. Don't worry at this stage about any gap in the return wall corner, and use a wood block and pencil as already described to trace across the board the actual line of the ceiling. The board can then be cut to this line to give a perfect fit at ceiling level. While somebody holds the board against the battens in its true position relative to the ceiling, you can use a block to scribe in the edge against the return wall, as described in the previous section. Scribe and cut each subsequent board in the same way, including the end of the final board, when you come to it.

If you are lining a fireplace wall, you may be faced with alcoves on either side of the chimney breast that are narrower than a standard width board and these should be fitted first. Measure across each alcove wall at top, centre and bottom, and cut the board to the narrowest of these measurements. Having cut it fractionally undersize, if need be, to clear floor and ceiling, and steps to sit over the skirting boards, scribe the board to the ceiling and fix in place. The gaps will be covered by the cladding on the side walls of the alcove.

The side walls forming the chimney breast should be covered next. Scribe the board to the ceiling then use the block and pencil to scribe the edge where it meets the cladding on the back wall of the alcove. The vertical batten on the corner of the chimney breast will give you a line to work to for cutting the front edge of the side cladding, though the pencil mark, being on the rear of the board, will have to be transferred to its face. Cut and fit this board; and line the other alcove before tackling the chimney breast.

If this is wider than 4 ft., you will have to adjust one full board and an offcut to get the best arrangement of vertical grooves. The ceiling-to-fireplace height is critical, because here you cannot hide a gap behind a skirting board. You would have to rely on a moulding pinned above the mantelpiece to hide any gap. If, in addition, your fire surround has an irregular shape, the difficulties in measuring, marking out and cutting accurately around them could be enough to stop even an experienced carpenter dead in his tracks at the limits of the alcove. He would probably suggest that madam settled for an architrave framing similar to that around the door to finish off the alcoves, and that the chimney breast should be papered or painted to complement the timber. In these circumstances, it could be a very sensible compromise for the amateur, too. If your fire surround is a simple rectangle, it shouldn't be an overwhelming problem to patch in around the surround, employing the scribing techniques with which by now you will be familiar. The alternative is to use narrow boards rather than sheet material, as single boards are easy to cut to size.

One final, vital point about timber cladding around a fireplace; it should never be taken right up to the grate opening. Commonsense would prevent you from doing this where an open coal fire is employed, but you could be tempted with an enclosed solid fuel stove or a built-in gas fire. In everybody's interests, you should check with the local council's surveyor's department before carrying out such work, but there is a basic rule you should bear in mind when planning alterations of this kind: Any heater with a metal casing that reaches a high temperature should be framed in a surround of incombustible material that is at least 1 in. wide. But local authority requirements vary – so don't take that as gospel.

Where veneered plywood boards are used to cover external angles, there will be exposed raw edges. The simplest way to cover them is with an angled moulding cover strip and such mouldings are normally stocked by big timber yards.

FIXING PLAIN HARDBOARD

If you are erecting standard plain hardboard, for subsequent painting or papering, there are other points to be observed. Standard hardboard is only $\frac{1}{8}$ in. thick, unlike the decorative simulated timber boards, and requires closer attention to fixing. First, it should be conditioned by wetting the mesh side as a precaution against warping. Brush into each 8×4 ft. sheet 1–2 pints of water, stack them flat, mesh to mesh, and leave to dry for 48 hours. This ensures that, after fixing, any movement will be shrinkage, resulting in tight, flat boards.

The boards should be nailed to a system of wall battens, as already described, at 4 in. intervals around the edges and 8-in. intervals over the rest of the battening. Having scribed the boards to follow the line of the walls, start nailing from the top and work downwards and outwards rather like brushing out wallpaper. This process will assist in avoiding bowing or buckling of the sheet. Use $\frac{5}{8}$ or $\frac{3}{4}$ in. panel pins and keep them about $\frac{3}{8}$ in. from the board edges. Buy 'lost head' pins, sometimes called hardboard nails, if you can. These have a diamond-shaped head which will be driven below the board surface by the hammer. Ordinary panel pins will have to be buried with a nail punch and the heads filled with a stopper.

Don't try to butt adjoining boards tightly together, for they might buckle eventually. When papering, you can leave slight gaps in the joints and cover them with plasterers' scrim, a sort of bandage obtainable from decorators' shops, bedded into a creamy mix of Sirapite, or a similar finishing plaster. With the scrim in position, apply another coat of finishing plaster and feather out the edges with a damp sponge to merge into the surface of the board. This treatment can also be used when the cladding is to be painted, but you will be very lucky if the joints between boards are undetectable after painting. If you prefer a painted finish, the best results will be obtained by treating the joints as described and applying a good quality lining paper to be painted.

Hardboards with a decorative finish can be nailed or glued to the battens, according to the type of finish. Those faced with hessian, vinyl or melamine, etc., should be glued, for panel pins would show on the surface. The only satisfactory way to glue them is to use a contact adhesive, but this takes quite a lot of skill. Contact adhesives are applied to both surfaces and allowed to dry before the surfaces are brought together. Once they are, the bond is immediate; you could not slide the board into its final position as you can with wallpaper and to place a board accurately first time takes a lot of experience.

Enamelled and melamine-finished boards with a tile effect can be pinned through the grooves and the nail heads covered disguised with a touch of white paint or a stopper such as Polyfilla. Moulded hardboards can be similarly treated; but use a wood stopper that matches the colour of the boards if you are going to varnish them.

TILING A WALL

A most important preliminary when tiling a wall is the setting out, because you will almost certainly be involved in cutting tiles at some point. The aim should be to avoid narrow strips where you can, and to place them in the least noticeable positions where you can't. With plain coloured tiles, the effect of cutting will not be so apparent, but if you choose one of the attractive arabesque or flowered designs that are becoming popular, the cutting is most important.

Setting out must be considered both horizontally, where the tiles finish in a corner, and vertically, between the skirting board and the uppermost row. Start by planning the horizontals, striking a vertical line with a plumb bob in the centre of the wall. From this point, you can either centre one tile on that line, or two tiles butting together on the line. Run out a 'dry' line of tiles by resting them on the skirting board using both methods to see how much of a cut tile you finish up with at the end. Choose the row that leaves you with the widest cut. If you find that you cannot avoid a thin strip – say less than half the width of a tile – adjust the position of the centred tile so that you will finish up with cut tiles of equal width at both ends.

Around doorways, window sills and similar places, a thin strip might be unavoidable and in such cases place the strips in the least conspicuous place.

If you have built-in fitments such as kitchen cupboards to tile round, make up a tiler's 'pinch rod'. This is simply a length of straight board marked out with pencilled divisions equal to the width of the tiles you are using, plus one-sixteenth of an inch between divisions to allow for grouting. Even an expert could become confused when taking a series of measurements for possible alternatives between obstructions, but with a pinch rod you can quickly discover where cut tiles will be involved between, say, a skirting board and wall mounted cupboards, and what adjustment to make. The pinch rod could also be used for planning horizontal runs, especially where they are broken by windows or other obstructions.

Wall tiling should start one tile up from the floor or skirting, plus the depth of any cut tile involved. (See Fig. 12.) Any cut tiles at either end of the wall should also be fitted last, so you start in the middle, working outwards and upwards. At the appropriate distance up from the floor, draw a pencil line against which to set the bottom edge of the first row to be laid. Obviously, this line must be quite straight, and you will need a spirit level and a long straight board. Set the board at the required height and stand the spirit level on top of it, adjusting the board as necessary until the bubble in the level is central. Then, without letting the board slip, draw your pencil line. (See Fig. 13.)

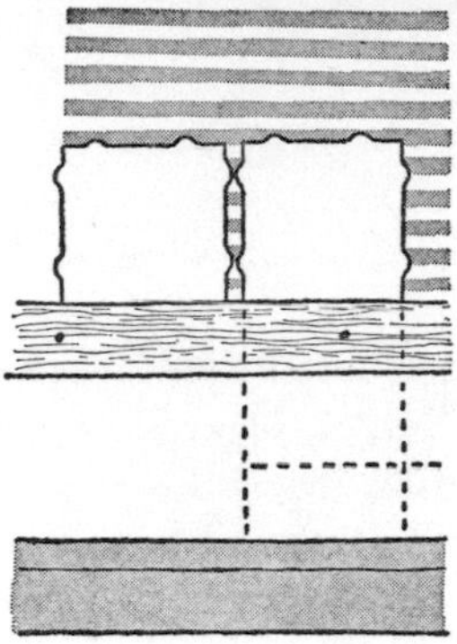

Fig. 12. The first row of wall tiles

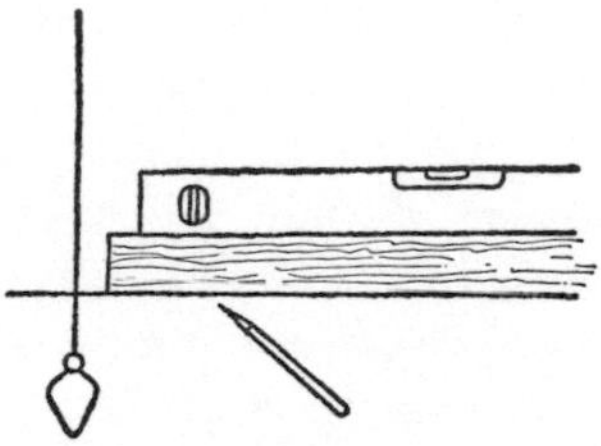

Fig. 13. Obtaining true guide lines

Against this line, tack a long wooden batten to the wall with masonry nails. The batten is necessary to support the tiles against sliding down the wall while the cement is hardening.

You are now ready to start tiling. Using a tile cement recommended by the tile maker, spread it on the wall over about 1 sq. yd. A serrated rectangular plasterer's trowel is best for this purpose, as it will build the cement into ribs which give a better key. If you don't want to buy this special trowel, you could use an existing rectangular trowel, filing a series of points along one edge a series of points about $\frac{1}{4}$ in. wide and $\frac{1}{4}$ in. deep.

Apply the tiles using firm finger pressure and see that the tiny spacer lugs on each tile butt together. When you have filled in the main area, you can trim in the finishing tiles.

The technique of cutting tiles accurately on the straight is soon learned. Make just one firm stroke of the cutter, ensuring that you nick through the glaze at the extreme edges of the tile. Extra strokes of the cutter won't help and they will blunt its edge. Lay the tile, glazed surface up, on a table edge or a block of wood with a sharp shoulder, and with the waste side of the cutting line just clear of the shoulder. Press down firmly and evenly on the piece to be broken off and it will sever in a clean line. Occasionally, there may be a small projection below the surface of the tile, but this is quickly removed with a coarse carborundum stone. To shape a curve, first cut away as much of the waste as you can with the cutter. The final shape can be achieved by crumbling away tiny pieces of tile with a pair of pincers. It's easy enough, if you don't dry to take large bites, and the final shaping can be given with the carborundum stone.

Where edge tiles run up against the obstruction of a door frame, skirting board, etc., take the measurement at either end of the gap carefully and transfer it to the tile. If the edge is out of square, the tiles will then follow the line of slope. Where tile edges will be exposed – at the top on a wall, around the corners of doorways and window sills, and so on – remember to calculate the quantities of tiles needed rounded on one or two edges as necessary.

Leave the bedding cement to dry overnight before grouting the joints between tiles. Use a recommended grouting cement, mixed to a creamy consistency. Allow it to stand for ten minutes before working it into the tile joints with a small pointing trowel, or stripping knife. Don't worry about smearing the paste over the surface of the tiles. When the job is complete, the surplus grout is scraped off with a small squeegee or piece of flat board. When the grout is dry, the white film over the surface will disappear quickly under a damp cloth.

FIXING METAL TILES

The principle of setting out metal tiles is exactly the same as for ceramic tiles but there are slight differences in fixing them. They do not need grouting because accurate edges can be machined in metal and they are therefore butted closely against each other. The adhesive should be smeared on the back of each tile with a small knife or trowel. Use a spirit based tile adhesive such as Dunlop CT-S if the tiles are likely to be constantly wet, as on a worktop, or a water based tile adhesive, such as Dunlop CT-W, in other circumstances. These tiles are usually finished with a brushed grain effect, so loose-lay a few first on a table, some with the grain running in the same direction and some with the grain of alternate tiles at right angles to their neighbours, to see which effect you prefer. You will find each tile protected with a clear plastic film which should be left in place to take any daubs of adhesive. Methylated spirits will remove any smears that do get on the tile surface. Use a small hacksaw for cutting the tiles and a file to finish any curves.

HANGING HESSIAN

As hessian is an open-weave material it is advisable first to paint the wall in a reasonably close colour match to the chosen shade, so that slight gaps between joints or plucks in the material will be camouflaged. To trim it to size, always use a very sharp blade because a blunt one would give a ragged cut. Holding the knife at a slight angle out from the straight-edge will also help to produce a clean cut. Don't pull frayed threads; use scissors or the trimming knife to remove them. To mark hessian for cutting, you can use a pencil, but a piece of tailor's chalk with a sharp edge is better. Re-roll each pre-cut length, and if the material tends to be springy, roll it in the opposite way to flatten it.

An ideal adhesive for hanging hessian that is easily available from decorators shops is Clam 143. Being of a stiff consistency, there is no need to worry about it seeping through the weave of the material. But it sets quickly, so you will have to work fast. Using a plumb line, snap a vertical chalk line to guide you in hanging the first piece. Cut the pieces to size leaving 3 in. surplus for trimming in, and apply the paste to the wall. Use a short bristled brush with which you can lay on heavily to draw this stiff adhesive out into a thin, even film. Take the first length of hessian, unroll the first foot and smooth it carefully into position by hand, allowing about half of the surplus to overlap the ceiling. Apply downwards and sideways pressure, but lightly because you don't want to stretch the material.

Once started, you can continue by rolling the material lightly against the wall from the open edge to the corner to push out any surplus. If you haven't a decorator's felt or rubber roller, you could adapt a paint roller by binding it tightly, with strips of clean cloth, until you have an even surface with no give in it. A less satisfactory alternative is a rolling pin. At this stage, keep the roller away from the open edge, so that you don't pick up adhesive and transfer it to the material.

Pull back the hessian to trim off any surplus in the corner with scissors and smooth back by hand, then roll it lightly again.

After about fifteen minutes, during which the adhesive will have begun to set and the material shrunk sufficiently, give it a final firm rolling and trim off the surplus at top and bottom, using a steel straightedge pressed tightly into the angles, and the trimming knife.

Brush adhesive on to the next strip of wall and smooth the hessian carefully into place, butting it against the previously hung piece, and rolling it outwards from there. After 15 minutes, trim in at top and bottom, and continue in this way with subsequent lengths.

FIXING ANAGLYPTA AND LINCRUSTA

Prepare the surface as described in Chapter 2 and size and line it. Low-relief Anaglypta is ready trimmed and is best hung with a starch paste, so be careful with the surface, as paste smears can stain. Paste, fold, and hang in the normal way. Sculptured Anaglypta panels need no underlining and should be fixed with a ready-mixed Dextrine paste, which is applied with a knife around the panel's edges and at the points where the embossed design touches the surface. Fixing will be made easier if you soak the panels in warm water first and hang them when almost dry.

Lincrusta should be fixed to a heavy duty lining paper. Cut each length exactly to size with a sharp trimming knife, sponge the back liberally with warm water and leave to soak for 20–30 minutes. Wipe off surplus moisture and apply W.K. glue. Don't be mean with it, and ensure all edges are well treated. You can soak several lengths at a time, but hang each length immediately it has been pasted. A hard rubber roller as used by decorators should be used to make it secure.

APPLYING TEXTURE PAINTS

Texture paints are sold in powder form in various quantities, from 1 lb. to 56 lb. bags. The powder is added to water and the consistency of the mix is governed by desired finish; the higher the relief required, the thicker the mix – that is the less water you add to the powder. It can be applied to any previously painted plaster wall, if the surface has to be cleaned and keyed as described in Chapter 2. Hair cracks will be covered by the texture paint as it is applied, but prominent cracks should be filled beforehand with some of the ready-mixed paint.

Slowly add the powder to the water, stirring all the time until you have mixed about half a bucketful. This is enough to start with while you are getting used to handling the material, though you will probably find that you can soon cope with larger mixes. The important thing, when applying the paint, is to keep the wet edges ragged, so that no joins are detectable between succeeding patches. If you can, persuade a friend to help, one of you applying the paint while the other follows on adding the textured effect.

Use a large, stubby paint brush or a trowel to apply the paint, covering one square yard at a time and working in the sequence for painting a wall described in Chapter 2. A variety of relief textures can be achieved with a sponge or long-bristled brush jabbed into the paint, twisted, dragged or gently dabbed. Experiment, first, on one patch to see which effect you like best. Tape newspaper around skirting boards door frames, etc., to keep the paint off them, because once it begins to harden, it will be difficult to remove entirely. When dry, treat it with a clear silicone water repellant which will help to keep dirt at bay, and make washing down easier in the future.

When the surface to be covered has a bold coloured finish to it, apply an undercoating of texture paint thinned to the consistency of emulsion paint. This will simultaneously blot out the old colour and provide a key for the finishing coat.

FIXING CEILING TILES

The best quality ceiling tiles are acoustic tiles made from fibre board, such as those produced in a variety of patterns and textures in the Armstrong Cushiontone and Celotex ranges. Some of them have a plastic paint finish, to make them easier to wipe down.

The best known, however, are those made from expanded polystyrene. These are mostly plain dappled white, though coloured and textured tiles are made, and the cheapest cost only a few pence each, compared with 2s. or more for fibre board tiles.

Standard tiles of both types are 12 in. sq. and are applied to the ceiling with adhesives. There are several special polystyrene adhesives, one of which your decorator's shop will stock, and fibre tile makers usually produce their own adhesives.

As with any tiling operation, you begin with an accurate setting-out of the area to be covered and the marking of accurate guide lines. First you must measure and mark the exact centre of each short end of the ceiling and snap a length of chalked string between the marks (coloured chalk, for clarity). Snap another chalk line across this from the centre points of the other two sides of the room.

On a ceiling, you start in one corner, so the next task is to work out reasonable borders of cut tiles of equal width. A narrow strip along one edge and a wide one along the other would look unsightly.

To calculate a tile border, take the odd inches of the room's width, add the width of one tile (12 in.) and divide the sum by two. For example, a room measures 11 ft. 6¾ in. wide at one end and 11 ft. 4⅛ in. at the other. Taking the widest of these, you would therefore halve 1 ft. 6¾ in., which would give a cut tile border at each end of 9⅜ in. maximum width, and an infill of ten complete 12 in. tiles.

Next, another chalk line will have to be snapped along the ceiling parallel to and 5 ft. from the centre line. This is your working line in one direction, and you must now use the same method to calculate the border tiles at the other two ends and to find the working line. Thus, there are guide lines close to the edge of the ceiling on one long end and one short end crossing in a corner at right angles to the other. To ensure that it is a true right angle, refer to Fig. 14. Make a mark on the longer

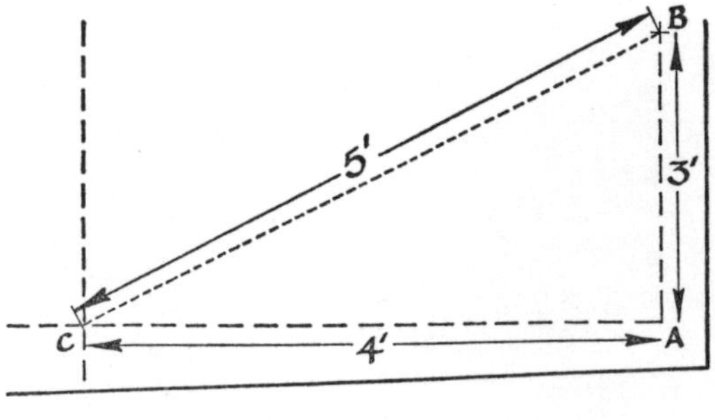

Fig. 14. Setting out a right angle

chalk line at a point exactly 3 ft. from the intersection of the two lines (A). Make another mark on the shorter chalk line 4 ft. from the intersection. Tie a pencil to a piece of string and get someone to hold the free end of the string 4 ft. away from the pencil and pressed against the intersection (A). With the string taut, scribe an arc over the shorter guide line (C). Now get your helper to hold the free end of the string 5 ft. from the pencil and place it on the 3 ft. mark (B), so you can scribe another arc to meet the first. The arcs should intersect on the shorter guide line, if the angle is a true 90 degrees. If it isn't, snap another chalk line which does intersect the arcs.

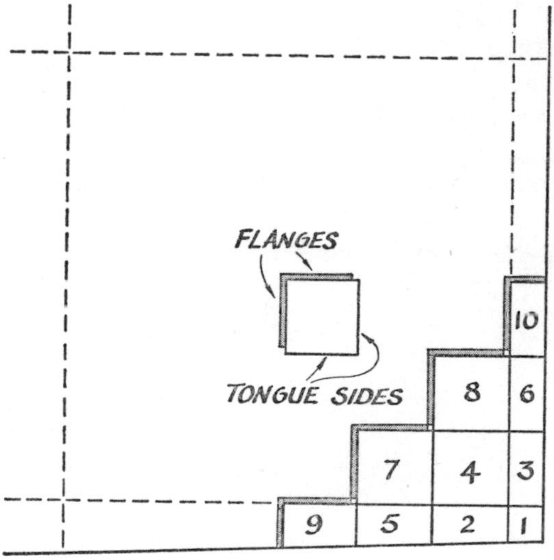

Fig. 15. Tiling a ceiling

You can now start tiling in this corner, working outwards in the sequence shown in Fig. 15. Each tile is grooved on two of its sides and tongued on the other two and the border tiles must be cut from the grooved sides and fixed with tongues facing outwards. To fix subsequent tiles, locate the tongues in the exposed grooves and press home with an upwards and sliding motion. Don't try to push the tiles flat against the ceiling; the adhesive is thick, and when it is sufficiently packed down the tile edges will be seen to be about $\frac{1}{8}$ in. clear of the ceiling.

Using a 2 in. stripping knife or similar spreader, apply the adhesive to each tile in the following manner: About 2 in. from each corner, spread a thin patch of adhesive, about 2 in. sq. Then scoop up on the spreader a quantity of adhesive and with a twirling motion, build up a mound, rather like a miniature whipped cream walnut, about 1 in. high on each of the patches.

Handle the tiles by their edges as much as possible, and to avoid unsightly finger marks, wear clean cotton gloves or keep the hands well dusted with french chalk or talcum powder. Acoustic tiles should be taken from their cartons and left to adjust to the normal room temperature for about 24 hours before fixing. They should be cut, face side up, with a sharp trimming knife, held at a slight outward angle so the tile is undercut. Make a light stroke with the knife first, then progressively heavier strokes to sever the tile.

Polystyrene tiles are handled in much the same way, but being fairly easily broken, and of soft density, need a little more care. A mortar board, made up from hardboard and scraps of timber to a size slightly less than that of the tile, is a useful tool for applying even pressure when positioning a tile.

Chapter 6: WHAT TO DO ABOUT FLOORS

SOUND FOUNDATIONS

Any good floor covering can be no better than its foundations allow, and while this statement must sound screamingly obvious, there's many a good floor covering been ruined by amateur laying – not because it's difficult, but because the rules have not been followed. The golden rule is to work on a surface that is dry, clean, free from grease, and reasonably level. Ignore it and all sorts of things can happen, such as tiles lifting, linoleum and carpets rotting or appearing after a few months to have been down for a couple of years.

Damp is the greatest menace because it is usually not apparent. Quarry tile and flagstone floors are still found frequently in old country properties and it is improbable that they have a damp course – an impervious vapour barrier – between them and the foundations beneath. In modern houses, a damp course will have been inserted in a concrete floor to join up with the damp course in the wall, but if the house is new, the surface concrete could still be damp. It takes at least two months for it to dry out, maybe longer if it was laid on a damp winter day. In flats and maisonettes, a lightweight concrete is used and this can take longer still. Such dampness is the usual cause of vinyl or linoleum tiles lifting, because the moisture breaks down the adhesive.

But it's an easy matter to determine whether a solid floor is dry. A quick way is to heat a metal plate about a foot square with a blow lamp or on a gas ring and place it on the bare floor to cool. When it is cool, a damp patch on the floor where it has lain and beads of moisture on the underside of the plate will tell you that the floor is damp. A slower test is to place panes of glass, vinyl tiles or pieces of lino face downwards on the floor and seal the edges with putty. Leave for 48 hours before lifting to see if there is any tell-tale moisture underneath. The damp test should be carried out at random spots all over the floor.

There are several ways in which you can damp proof a floor yourself, depending on the kind of finish chosen. A loose-laid covering of sheet vinyl, lino or matting could be protected from rising damp with an underlay of 500-gauge polythene sheet which should be turned three or four inches up the walls.

For a permanently laid flooring, you will have to make a damp proof membrane and lay on top of that a stable sub-floor. The damp course could be either a sheet of 500 gauge polythene, or you could brush on to the floor two or three coats of a bituminous damp-proofer, such as Synthaprufe or Aquaseal. If the floor is fairly level, you could then bed into this a sub-floor of plywood or chipboard. If you do, make sure that the edges of the sub-floor are sealed by carrying the membrane up the walls for three or four inches, or, if there is a damp course in the house walls, to a height where it can be joined to the damp course.

Before any kind of tiles are laid, the sub-floor must be level and perfectly smooth. There isn't much you will be able to do about a pronounced slope in a floor, but it must be free from bumps, hollows and cracks, and mostly you will be able to achieve this condition with a sub-floor of chipboard or plywood laid on a very rough solid floor. Timber floors we will deal with in a moment.

A smooth and reasonably level concrete floor can be made damp-proof ready for tiles by applying a coat of a hard setting damp-proofer such as Structoplast, making sure that it is worked well into any cracks. A levelling compound such as Plycolay should then be used to fill in any depressions and left to harden.

Boarded floors must also be made smooth and level and any dampness, which you could find in kitchens and bathrooms, allowed to dry out. Secure all loose floorboards and hammer protruding nail heads well down below the board surface. If the floor is otherwise in good condition – no gaps between boards, no rough surfaces, or splintered edges, no undue spring in the boards as you walk across them – the floor should need no more preparation. If, however, the boards are badly

ABOVE: Steam resistant and washable vinyl wallpapers are ideal for bathroom and kitchen. This is Shoal, a fish motif in ICI's Vymura range. BELOW: Sanderson fabrics and Crown wallpapers come in a wide range of pattern-matched designs for continuity of decoration

ABOVE: Modern printing processes have captured realistic looking stone walls, timber panelling and even animal skins on paper. These three are all in the Crown range. BELOW: Plywood panelling in many exotic veneers is now widely available. This is a walnut grained panel called Traditional in the Abitibi Classic series

worn and there are large gaps showing between boards, the whole floor will have to be covered before you can lay any floor covering satisfactorily.

Hardboard makes an excellent foundation for any kind of decorative covering. It should be laid in 2 ft. or 4 ft. sq. panels, arranged so that the joints are staggered, and fixed with $\frac{3}{4}$ in. ring nails spaced at 4 in. round the edges of a board and at 6 in. intervals within the board area. Panel pins will do, but ring nails, which have circular grooves around the shanks, will grip better, resisting any tendency to work loose as a board flexes underfoot.

The hardboard panels should be conditioned first by brushing clean water into the mesh side – about $\frac{3}{4}$ pt. per 4 ft. board – and leaving them stacked flat, mesh to mesh, for 48 hours. When laying, butt adjoining boards together without force and then fill any gaps with a cellulose filler.

Treating a timber floor in this way is going to seal off any upwards air circulation there may have been, so it is vital to ensure that airbricks providing ventilation to the floor joists are not blocked, or you could end up with a severe case of dry rot. There's another hazard you could find in a house built up to the turn of the century: Frequently, builders constructed timber ground floors directly on bare earth. If you think this could apply to yours, take up a floorboard and have a look, and consult a builder before sealing off a timber floor laid on bare earth.

THE CHOICE IN CARPETS

The day Man discovered that the skin of a sabre-tooth tiger was pleasant to sit on was the day that carpets came to stay. Mrs Caveman might argue that there was nothing like a hard rock floor for keeping clean and that the skin would attract the sabre-tooth mouse, but comfort began, that day, to prevail over function, and we are the beneficiaries. Although we accept unquestioningly the virtues of carpets, we are today assailed by a bewildering selection of materials and types of carpet, quite apart from the choice of colours and patterns. To make the right buy, we should know something of what's in store for us when we visit the carpet shop.

Most of us know the terms, Wilton and Axminster, tufted and cord, but discerning shoppers can get themselves a better deal by knowing the easily understood, basic facts about modern carpets.

Woven carpets are the traditional types, best known by the names Wilton and Axminster, which are used to describe a type of weave. With Wiltons, you get an almost infinite choice of plain colours; you could even have your own made up for very little extra cost. Manufacturers also produce a wide choice of sculptured designs, that is three-dimensional effects, through cutting the pile at varying heights. But Wilton looms can handle no more than about five colours at a time and this limits the range of patterns offered. Axminster looms can handle any number of colours, so it is in this type of carpet that you find the widest variety of patterns. They are also able to weave all sorts of sculptured effects. The pile of an Axminster carpet is always cut and that of Wiltons usually so, though Wilton construction is also used in cord carpets. Domestically, these are generally at the inexpensive end of the scale, employing cheaper man-made fibres and animal hair. Notwithstanding, they are hard wearing because the tight-looped weaving process gives them a resilience they otherwise wouldn't have. Woollen corded Wiltons, often called Brussels carpets, are priced well up in the luxury class.

Tufted carpets were developed for their low manufacturing costs, and inexpensive tufteds can represent good value for bedrooms and similar little-used areas. But manufacturing techniques have improved to the point where, at the top end of the price scale, tufteds will give you every bit as much wear as a woven carpet of equal quality and probably cost less. To the untrained eye, there is also no visible difference. The serious limitation with tufted carpets compared with the woven variety is the available choice of colours and patterns, the latter generally being confined to speckled and mottled effects and a few crude patterns.

The crucial consideration in any carpet is its wearing properties and these are governed by the materials from which it is made. Several types of fibre can be used, and usually, two or three are blended to balance durability and cost. Wool, the traditional fibre, is soft and resilient, resists soiling and is very durable. Nylon, on the other hand, is tougher, easier to clean and cheaper than wool, though it soils more readily. Most manufacturers make carpets from a blend of both materials. Percentages vary, but it is commonly 80 per cent wool, and 20 per cent nylon in a good quality carpet. Evlan and Evlan M are cheaper man-made forms of reinforced rayon developed for carpet making, and these are also used in blending less expensive carpets which are nevertheless attractive and hardwearing. Relative newcomers are the acrylic fibres, Acrilan and Courtelle. These both closely approach wool in feel and resilience and are extremely hard wearing. An additional advantage is that they do not absorb liquids and therefore spillages are quickly dealt with. They don't resist dirt as readily as wool, but they are easier to clean. Cord carpets, made from sisal or blends of wool and animal hair, make good budget carpets when one considers price and durability. The range of colours is limited but subtle and simple patterning is obtainable. Compared with the other fibres, sisal carpeting is somewhat unsympathetic to the touch, but claims of at least ten years wear are not uncommon.

The range of carpet sizes is extremely wide. Body carpet for laying on stairs and along corridors starts at 18 in. though the choice in this size is not very large. But between 27 in. and 54 in. there is plenty of choice both in colour and pattern. Broadloom weaves start at 6 ft. and go up to 15 ft., so it is possible to close carpet a fairly large room with a seamless piece.

However, there are circumstances where 27 in. or 36 in. body carpet would prove a better choice. Where a room has many recesses created by alcoves, bay windows and projecting walls, a narrower carpet could be the most economical way of close carpeting. Also, manufacturers often try out new designs in the narrower widths first, and trendsetters will find more scope here, therefore. Carpet squares with purpose-made patterns are produced in standard dimensions between $2\frac{1}{2} \times 2$ yds. and 5×4 yds.

Carpets employing new manufacturing techniques developed for mass production of contract carpeting of great durability and ease of maintenance for rough-and-tumble installations in schools, hotels and the like are now establishing a place on the domestic scene, as something half-way between carpet and vinyl or lino. They are called bonded carpets and are made from polypropylene, nylon, and other man-made fibres and because of their toughness and water repellancy, you could use them in kitchens, bathrooms and similar places where you would hesitate to lay conventional carpet. They are without pile, like a felt, though some have a dimpled surface to add textural interest and depth. Most of them are intended to be stuck to the floor, though they can be loose laid. Colour choice is limited to about a dozen colour tones, most of them of the neutral values that architects and interior designers tend to go for.

A development of much greater domestic interest is carpet tiles. Aesthetically they can be pleasing; functionally, they are the ideal flooring for families that move home frequently. They are simple for the householder to lay himself, even as a fitted carpet, and with the loose-laid type, they are easy to lift, pack and relay in a new home. It is unlikely that a fitted carpet will adapt readily to a new room, and carpet tiles offer much more scope for solving this problem. And if you haven't got enough for a larger room, all you have to do is buy some more, either matching or in another colour, to make a contrasting border.

Carpet tiles also solve the problem of evening-out wear; you merely change from time to time a few of the tiles in areas of heavy wear with those in out-of-the-way corners. Upset a drink on a tile and you can lift it and deal with the damage comfortably at the kitchen sink. If a stain is irremovable, you have ruined a tile, not a carpet; it can be banished under the settee.

Despite one's instinctive suspicions, loose-laid carpet tiles really do hug the floor and won't kick up or otherwise be dislodged except by deliberately prising them loose with a finger and thumb. They are cleaned and maintained in the normal way. They are available with a soft nylon cut pile or a shaggy goat hair pile that is quite pleasing to the eye. The colour range is again limited to those shades that are top of the architect's hit parade. There is another kind of tile, made by the methods already described for bonded carpets, and these must be stuck down and are treated with a self-adhesive backing for this purpose.

Tiles don't need an underlay but most carpets do, though some manufacturers are now making them with built-in foam rubber underlays.

If you choose hessian-backed carpet, it is false economy not to provide an underlay. It acts as a cushion between the carpet and floors that are hard, rough or uneven. It will also protect the carpet against the infiltration of dust through cracks in floorboards, absorb a lot of the pressure on the carpet pile from heavy furniture, and add the final, luxurious, springy touch to the carpet. In these and other ways, it can double the life of a carpet.

Convinced? Well, which kind of underlay? A good quality felt product has lots of resilience and will allow body carpeting to bed down at the seams so that they are barely visible. A rubber underlay, with its millions of microscopic air bubbles, will give a spring to the carpet that is luxurious to feel underfoot. A combination of felt bonded to a foam backing will combine the best characteristics of both. On staircases, underlay pads of felt or rubber should be used on each tread. Pads can be bought for the purpose, or you can cut them from a length of material to the width of the tread, plus about 2 in. to turn and tack under the nosing of the tread.

All the foregoing is the sort of information you will be sifting when selecting the quality of carpet. You will be juggling cost with quality, adding the expense of underlay, or allowing this cost against a carpet with built-in underlay, trying to assess the wear, convenience, comfort and pleasure it's going to give you, and so on. And these are certainly the key questions about which you have to be satisfied before saying 'Deliver it on Saturday.' However, there are a few other considerations you should take into account before you make up your mind:

Spend a little bit more than you think you can afford on carpets for the living room, staircase, and any other areas where the going could be rough. If you have to economise, do so on bedroom carpets, which get little wear.

By all means go into raptures over a particular shade of self-coloured carpet. But remember that it will mercilessly expose crumbs, dog hairs, threads and similar flotsam, and could turn you into a compulsive carpet sweeper. Patterned carpets, on the other hand, will camouflage these for a long time, and will 'digest' spillages and other accidents far more readily than plain carpet can.

Don't go overboard for a lovely pattern; just because it's a lovely pattern. Maybe your walls have got lovely patterns, too.

And the curtains. And the furniture upholstery. Remember that they all have to live together, for your sake.

For most of us, wall-to-wall carpeting is the last word in flooring luxury, but we have to accept the fact that it cannot be turned occasionally to even out wear. If the head of the household is a career man, whose future involves frequent changes of residence, you might be better off buying the best carpet squares you can afford and dealing as simply as you can with the surrounding floor.

If you have read all we've said about weaves, fibres and blends, you must acknowledge that, in the end, you are at the mercy of the carpet salesman. In an open market place or a one-day 'flood salvage sale' this could be a long-lasting source of regret to you. But if you deal with a retailer who is here today and is not going to be on fire tomorrow, the basic knowledge you have gained from reading this will carry you through. He wants you back – but to buy more carpet – not to create a scene about the carpet you have already bought.

Life being what it is, you can still get a dim salesman in a reputable shop, but you are still not on your own . . . Look on the backs of the carpets or samples that interest you, and you will probably find two or three labels, which are guarantees of quality. On the backs of the majority of woven carpets will be the label of the British Carpet Centre which will state the general usage for which that particular carpet is suitable (light, medium and heavy), and the maker's name. It will also include a guarantee against defective materials and workmanship. Leading brands of tufted carpets will be covered by the Teltag Scheme, sponsored by the Government-backed Consumer Council. This is even more informative and consists of a label showing all the essential information – where to use that particular brand of carpet, what it's made of, what sizes are available, how it stands up to shampooing, and so on. The Teltag Scheme applies also to rugs. Some of the bigger carpet manufacturers also operate their own labelling schemes, in addition. Kosset, for example, has a colour coded label system that is somewhat complex – Nairn Velmar use a code of chevrons that is easy to follow, and some fibre manufacturers (Monsanto, for example, who produce Acrilan) issue their own labels to approved carpet manufacturers.

Finally, a word about fitting carpets yourself. There are no difficulties that a man of average ability cannot overcome in laying staircarpet, but it would be false economy to by-pass the professional where good quality close-carpeting in a room is involved. Experience and special tools are needed to achieve the even tension that is necessary. If there's too little or an uneven stretch, creases and patchy wear will result; over-stretching could weaken the carpet. But it's difficult to create serious damage in fitting one of the cheaper grade tufted carpets yourself in such places as bedrooms, so let's see what's involved in laying a fitted carpet and a staircarpet.

FITTED CARPET

You will make life easier for yourself if you choose broadloom tufted carpet. Broadloom because its 15-ft. width should eliminate seams; or reduce them to one. Tufted, because it will cut without the edges fraying. The carpet should be firmly anchored around its perimeter and the common ways of doing this are by folding over a hem and tacking it at frequent intervals, or by hooking the carpet over proprietary fixings generally called tackless grippers. These consist of lengths of metal or plywood strips incorporating lots of angled short spikes that grip the carpet backing. (See Fig. 16.) Many carpet suppliers stock these, under such brand names as Cimco, Smoothedge and Invisigrip, and they provide an even, hidden anchorage.

Gripper strips are nailed or screwed around the perimeter of the room, and can be cut into short lengths to follow the profiles of fireplaces, alcoves, window bays, etc. They should

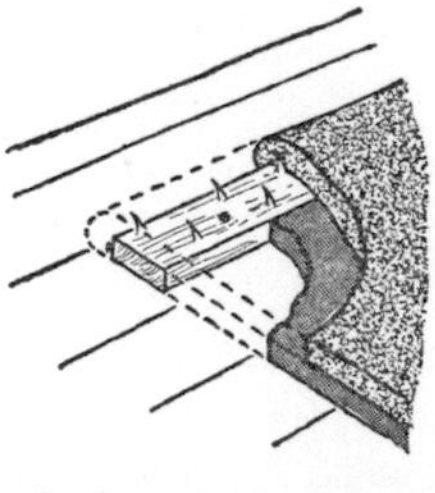

Fig. 16. Securing a fitted carpet

be fixed about ¼ in. from the wall or skirting, a gap needed eventually to tuck away the carpet edge.

Once the gripper strip is fitted, the underlay should be stretched and tacked into position. Tack a foamed rubber underlay right up to the gripper strip at one end and a felt underlay ½ in. away from the strip to allow for bedding down. Stretch the underlay tight across the floor, forwards and sideways, and tack as you go. At the opposite end, trim off the surplus, then lay succeeding lengths in the same way. If covering a boarded floor, an initial layer of paper felt will make a worthwhile and inexpensive dust barrier. It can be secured to the floor with random dabs of adhesive.

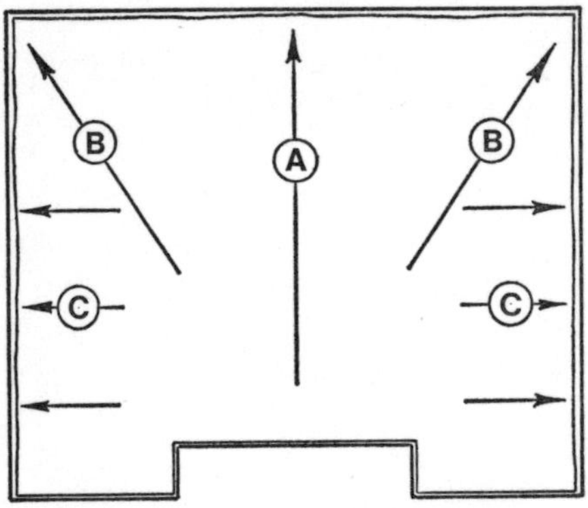

Fig. 17. Stretching a fitted carpet

Next, cut the carpet roughly to shape and about 2 in. oversize all round. Starting along the fireplace or other main wall of the room, press the carpet firmly on to the pins of the gripper strip, leaving about 1 in. of surplus carpet turned up against the wall. From this centre point, stretch the carpet straight across to the opposite wall and fix it at the central point. (See Fig. 17.) Then continue stretching it diagonally to the corners on either side of that central, opposite point, pressing it on to the gripper pins as you go. Finally, stretch the carpet at right angles from the central axis towards each opposite wall and secure it to the gripper pins. When the carpet is hooked all round over the gripper pins, you should then go round and trim the surplus riding up the walls, leaving about $\frac{1}{4}$ in. surplus, which is tucked between the gripper strip and the wall.

In an L-shaped room, or similar situation where two pieces of carpet have to be joined together, use a backing strip of hessian about 3 in. wide and coat it with a latex adhesive such as Copydex. Butt-joint the pieces of carpet on to the hessian strip and leave to dry for at least half an hour before attempting to stretch and fit that section of the carpet.

LAYING A STAIRCARPET

On a straight run of staircase, fitting a carpet is quite easy, and indeed you will be relaying it yourself about twice a year after the initial laying, if you want to avoid uneven wear of the pile. If there are three or four 'winders' – triangular-shaped stairs that turn a corner – the operation is slightly more complicated. In such cases, it's best to drop any idea of close-carpeting the stairs and choose a standard width of carpet that leaves a few inches of exposed stairs on either side. As you will see later, there will be surplus carpet to be tucked out of sight on winders and as you cannot do this with close carpeting, separate pieces would have to be cut and fitted to the winders. Thus you would run into trouble each time you came to adjust the carpet for wear. Add to the actual length of carpet needed about another $\frac{1}{2}$ yd. for periodic repositioning.

Gripper strip should be nailed to the riser and tread of each stair but you can omit a strip on the riser from the hall and, at this stage on the riser of each winding stair. The pins on the tread strip should point towards the riser immediately above it, and the pins on that riser point downwards to the tread. The strips should be fixed about $\frac{1}{2}$ in. from the angle between them. Underlay or pre-cut stairpads should be tacked to the treads and stretched and tacked just below the nosing of each tread.

Start laying the carpet from the bottom stair and have the pile pointing downwards. Stroke a hand across the carpet to discover which way the 'grain' runs. Double under the first riser a length of surplus and tack it into position. Stretch the carpet tightly over the first tread and force it between the jaws made by the gripper strips, hammering it into place with a blunt wooden wedge to ensure a firm fixing on the pins. Carry

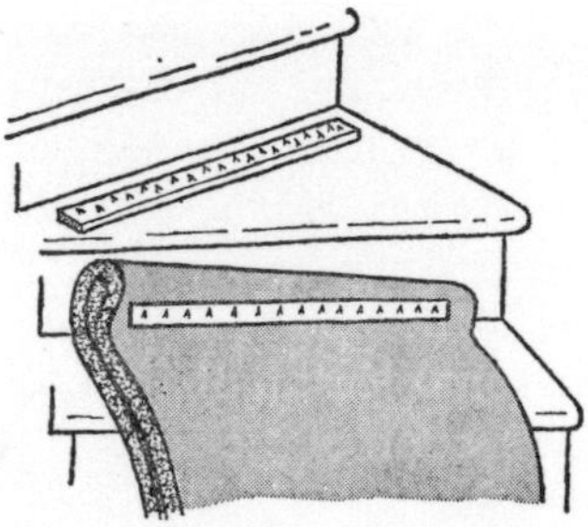

Fig. 18. Fitting a staircarpet

on like this until you come to the first winder. Referring to Fig. 18, stretch the carpet tightly across the tread of the first winder and double the carpet back under the next riser. Nail into the fold a length of gripper strip, using 2 in. nails to pass through both thicknesses of carpet into the staircase. Hook the carpet tightly up over the riser, stretch it over the next tread. Repeat the procedure on subsequent winders, and terminate the carpet immediately under the nosing of the riser to the landing. The remaining surplus can and should be doubled under, as at the bottom of the stairs, for use in future adjustments.

CARPET CARE

For the first few weeks of a new carpet's life, use a stiff brush to clean it once a day, moving in the direction of the pile. At this stage, the carpet will continually shed fluff, but this is normal and will eventually cease. When it does, you can start daily vacuum cleaning. If you skimp this task, grit will gradually become embedded in the pile. Being abrasive, it will shorten the carpet life if allowed to remain.

Eventually, the carpet will need cleaning and proprietary do-it-yourself carpet shampoos will give satisfactory results for a long time. But the day will come when deep shampooing by experts will be necessary, and how soon will depend on how the carpet has been treated, and the atmosphere where you live. If in doubt, part the carpet pile and look at the fibres under a torch. If discoloration goes deep, you won't clean the carpet successfully yourself.

STAIN	CLEANER*
Alcoholic drinks	Water and detergent
Animal and children waste	Water and detergent followed (if needed) by bleach solution and water
Blood	Plain water
Butter	Water and detergent
Chewing gum	Soften with dry cleaning solvent and scrape
Coffee	Water and detergent
Egg	Plain water, or water and detergent
Fruit juices	Water and detergent followed (if needed) by bleach solution and water
Furniture polish	Dry cleaning solvent
Glue (carpenter's) (dope cement) (resin type)	Water and detergent followed by warm water Acetone Plain water
Ink	Water and detergent followed (if needed) by bleach solution and water
Iodine	Sodium thiosulphate (hypo) solution (from the chemists) followed by water and detergent
Lipstick	Dry cleaning solvent followed by water and detergent
Machine oil	Dry cleaning solvent
Mayonnaise	Water and detergent
Milk	Water and detergent
Mustard	Water and detergent
Nail polish	Nail polish remover
Rust	Oxalic acid solution (salts of lemon). Rinse well with water and detergent. It may take several applications and an old stain may need professional attention. Beware – oxalic acid is poisonous.
Shoe cream	Water and detergent followed (if needed) by bleach solution and water
Shoe polish (wax)	Dry cleaning solvent followed (if needed) by bleach solution and water
Soft drinks	Water and detergent
Sweets	Water and detergent followed (if needed) by dry cleaning solvent
Tar	Dry cleaning solvent
Tea	Water and detergent
Urine	Water and detergent. May need several applications
Wax candles and crayons	Dry cleaning solvent followed (if needed) by water and detergent

* Detergent here refers to proprietary carpet shampoos; dry cleaning solvent, preparations such as Thawpit, and bleach a solution of a domestic bleach diluted with ten parts water.

When accidents happen, deal with them straight away. Gently scrape up as much as you can of any solids, then treat the spillage according to the directions given in our first aid chart on page 75. Always use clean, white absorbent material, such as a piece of old bedsheet, and dab – don't rub or brush a stain. Work from the outer edge to the centre. Some solvents, such as carbon tetrachloride should not be used on rubber-backed carpets so if you are using a proprietary solvent, read the label carefully before applying it.

THE CHOICE IN VINYL AND LINO

Since the early post war introduction of plastic tiles, this type of flooring material has been developed to a point where it has almost pushed linoleum out of the domestic market. Most of those first stodgy brown tiles will by now have been given a decent burial under a more attractive floor covering, for they were not all that satisfactory when compared with their modern counterparts. They were hard and unsympathetic to walk on, prone to crack, and did not have a great resistance to wear and spillages. These were called thermoplastic or asphalt tiles and made basically from asbestos.

Then came vinyl asbestos tiles, still a good seller and a great improvement on the former, offering a brighter, wider range of colours, a good resistance to abrasion, indentation and spillages, and the opportunity to lay them yourself, which thermoplastic tiles didn't. The asbestos content also gives them some resistance to burning by cigarettes, hot cinders, etc., but scuffs from rubber-soled shoes are difficult to remove.

But the biggest advances have been in flexible vinyl floorings, which can be obtained in tile and sheet form. Vinyl is quieter and nicer to walk on, and, though easily damaged by dropped cigarettes, it is generally harder wearing and infinitely easier to maintain than linoleum, which needs frequent polishing as well as cleaning. We will look a little closer at qualities in a moment, for the really exciting aspect of vinyls is the tremendous choice of decorative effects they offer.

In the better quality tiles, you can find marbled effects that are virtually undetectable by eye from the real thing; tiles moulded into realistic three-dimensional imitations of smooth-pebbled patios, bricks, terra-cotta and mosaic tiles, and even riven blue slate. Some of these effects are also available in sheet form, with the design 'floating' in clear, glass-smooth vinyl.

In the cheaper and more popular sheet vinyls, photographic processes have given designers free reign on the patterns they can produce, which can vary from the hot kaleidescopes seen in seaside snackbars, to cool reproductions of classical courtyards.

Another recent development is cushioned vinyl, a material with a built-in underlay, and many built-in advantages. It will not shrink in length or as most vinyls do. Because it is resilient, it offers greater resistance to the impact of any stiletto heels that are still around, and the legs of heavy furniture. Because it is stable, it can be loose-laid where other vinyls have to be stuck down – along the seams, at least. The composition of cushioned vinyls produces in most cases a slightly textured surface which makes them safe underfoot where smooth vinyls tend to be slippery when wet. And cushioned vinyls make a floor softer, quieter and warmer to walk on.

What, you may ask, has happened to linoleum, and the short answer is that it is still around to give you a harder wearing floor at a little greater cost, in certain circumstances. In terms of durability, sheet lino will outlast the popular, gaily-patterned grades of domestic quality vinyls. These, as we have said, are treated with a very thin coating of clear vinyl, whereas good domestic quality lino is at least 2 mm. thick and solid to its backing. But it needs more care and cleaning and polishing than vinyls do. In better quality furnishing stores, you will find heavier grades of vinyl around 2·5 mm. thick. These are used extensively for contract work and will outlast lino of equivalent thickness. Domestic quality lino tiles are about the same thickness as their vinyl counterparts, which are therefore more durable.

LAYING TILES

Tiles, whether vinyl or lino, must be stuck down with an adhesive recommended by the manufacturer, though some producers of vinyl tiles, Dunlop and Nairn, for instance, make self-adhesive tiles. These are entirely suitable for domestic situations and for a slight extra cost cut out the messy, extra operation of applying adhesive to the floor. With some, you peel a protective paper backing from each tile, thus exposing the adhesive; with others, each tile is dipped into a bowl of water for a few seconds to activate the adhesive.

The sub-floor should be prepared as described earlier. Tiles can be stuck directly to a smooth and level concrete floor or one that has been covered with hardboard. On a boarded floor in good condition, stick to the boards a thick paper underlay, then stick the tiles to that. Sweep the sub-floor clean of any grit before laying the underlay, and sweep again before laying the tiles. Any loose fragments could cause high spots in the tiles and might eventually wear through to the surface.

But the first job when laying tiles is to mark out the prepared floor. The walls are unlikely to run exactly parallel and adjoining walls to be exactly at right angles, and if you were to use the wall as a guide, you would almost certainly finish up with a tiled surface visibly out of alignment. You must therefore measure and mark the centre of the floor at one end of the room, do the same at the other, and connect these two marks by snapping a length of chalked string against the floor to make a true guide line. At right angles to this across the width of the room, snap another chalk line in the centre.

Place a tile on one side or the other of the angle formed by these lines and loose-lay a row of tiles along each, to form an 'L.' If, at the end of either row you are left with a small gap which will have to be filled with a cut tile, the guide lines will have to be adjusted. Assuming that you find a narrow gap at the end of each row, move the centre or key tile over to a point where you can lay out the tiles again and finish up with a gap at each end of approximately the width of half a tile. Mark on the floor the new position of the key tile, measure its distance from the original guide lines and mark these measurements at each end of the guide lines. Now you can mark the new guide lines and are ready to lay the tiles.

That is the method by which you ensure that your tiles run true and it's a straightforward operation in rectangular room. But where the outline is complicated by built-in cupboards, sink units and the like, you might have to shuffle the loose rows of tiles about quite a bit to find the arrangement that gives you the maximum width of cut tile around the fittings and along the wall.

The adhesive for dry tiles should be applied to the floor a square yard at a time, using a serrated spreader to form the adhesive into ribs. Wait until it is just tacky before laying the tiles; the warmer the room, the quicker the adhesive will dry. For the first square yard, spread it carefully to avoid obliterating the chalk marks, so that you have a clear sight line to work to. As the first tiles are laid to the line, scrape the appropriate edges lightly across the patch of adhesive, as this will pick up sufficient adhesive to bond that edge to the dry guide line.

You are working with a contact adhesive, which means that the tiles cannot be slid into their final position or adjusted once they are down, so take great care to align the key tile accurately. Offer it up into the chosen corner of the bisecting guide lines and lay it from that corner outwards, using firm hand pressure. Working to the longer guide line, butt one edge of a second tile against the key tile so that it registers exactly, then press it in place. Lay two more tiles to the long guide line, then work outwards in the same way from this row of tiles until a square yard has been completed. A wooden hand roller, or rolling pin should then be worked over the area. Clean up any seepage of adhesive with a solvent recommended by the manufacturer as you go, and continue in this sequence to complete the main area of the floor.

The usual recommendation is to lay alternative tiles with the marble flecks running at right angles to those of adjacent tiles. This is said to produce the best effect, but this cannot be a positive assertion, and you might prefer the look of them with the flecks running in a continuous parallel pattern.

Leave cutting-in round the edges until last and stick to the following method, to be sure of a perfect fit with every tile you cut. Referring to Fig. 19a, place a loose tile on the last full tile in the row so that it registers exactly. Take a spare tile as a guide for cutting. The shaded portion is the piece to be fitted (Fig. 19b).

Cut along the line with a sharp trimming knife for vinyl. For lino, the traditional hooked blade (which should also be sharp) is better. If you make a deep score, a tile will break

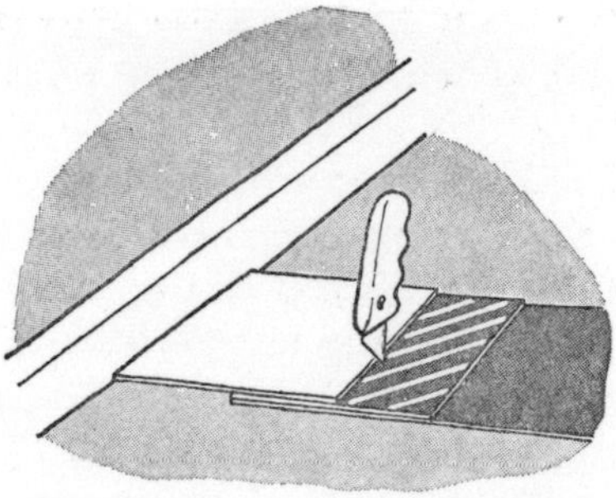

Fig. 19a. Marking an edge floortile

cleanly when folded back. When positioning the tile to be cut, remember to place it with the marbling running in the appropriate direction.

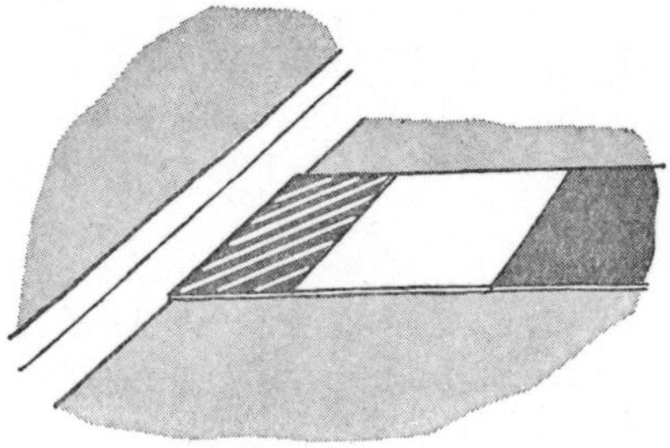

Fig. 19b. The edge tile in place

Tiling that stops in a doorway should terminate at a point half-way under the door, so that it is seen from the room side with the door closed, but not the other. Fig. 20 shows how to trim-in round a door's architraves. Lay the tile to be cut on the last complete tile within the door opening and use a spare tile to mark the various distances as the moulding changes shape. Then lay the marked tile on the last complete tile just inside the door and make a similar series of marks. When these are joined up, you will have the exact shape of the moulding to cut to.

Fig. 21 shows how to cut round central heating pipes and similar obstructions. The tile to be cut is positioned on the last full tile in front of the pipe and a tile used to mark the surplus.

Another tough, washable vinyl with a kitchen motif, ICI's Vymura Gourmet design is shades of pink and mustard on a white background

For the nursery, Donkey Serenade is a Crown Cleenstrip vinyl coated paper. It's washable and is quickly peeled off the wall when redecoration is needed.

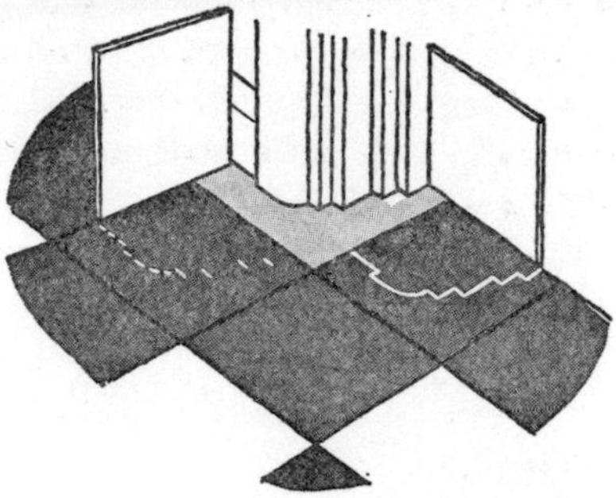

Fig. 20. Using a tile to mark out round a door

When this has been removed, place the tile again so that the thickness and position of the pipe can be marked on it. Draw those lines down to a position equal to the distance of the pipe from the wall, cut a hole to accommodate the pipe diameter, then cut the tile through once from the hole to the back. It can be opened and fed round the pipe for sticking down.

If you have electric underfloor heating, turn the heating off 48 hours before you start laying the tiles and leave it off for another 48 hours when the floor is complete. This is to prevent the adhesive being affected by heat. Avoid high floor temperatures for about a week afterwards.

The fitting of cork tiles is basically the same, though a

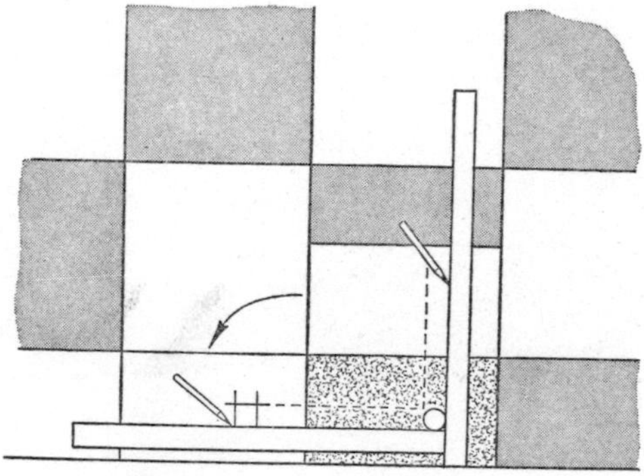

Fig. 21. Marking tiles for cutting round pipes

contact adhesive that is applied to both sub-floor and tile is usually recommended by the makers. Spread it thinly on the backs of the tiles and leave till touch dry. When it is, the tiles can be stacked vertically against a wall, out of the way.

Stack them with a coated side touching a surface side; if stacked back to back, the adhesive would bond at points of contact. The sub-floor can then be coated with adhesive and left to dry.

LAYING SHEET VINYL AND LINO

Prepare the sub-floor as already described and sweep thoroughly to remove grit and splinters, etc., before laying starts. A paper underfelt is needed on floor boards in good condition, but it can be loose-laid. The felt will ride over any expansion and contraction of the boards and help to prevent the floorcovering from becoming lined by the boards. Lay the felt against the way it has been rolled so that it hugs the floor, and lay it at right angles to the floor boards, butt-joined at the edges.

Vinyl and lino are at their most pliable for cutting and laying when at room temperature, so first loosen the roll and leave in a warm room for a few hours before starting.

Starting at the doorway, measure the distance between walls and cut the first length allowing about 4 in. of surplus for trimming in to the skirting. Lay the piece so that it turns up the wall at each end. Referring to Fig. 22, measure the distance

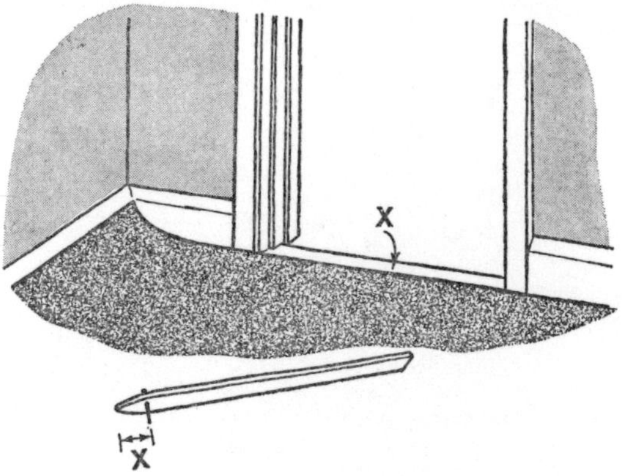

Fig. Setting the scribing bar

from the edge across the doorway to a point on the threshold which would be half-way under the door when closed. That distance must be set on a scribing bar, which the tradesmen use to score guide lines in the surface of the material, and which you can make easily from about 2 ft. of wood strip and a nail. If the distance into the threshold from the edge of the material is 1½ in., the nail would be set 1½ in. from the tip of the bar, and the surface of the sheet scratched to follow the profile of the door mouldings (See Fig. 23.) When this has been done on either side of the door frame and the marks joined up in pencil, the surplus material can be cut out, and the length slid snugly into position.

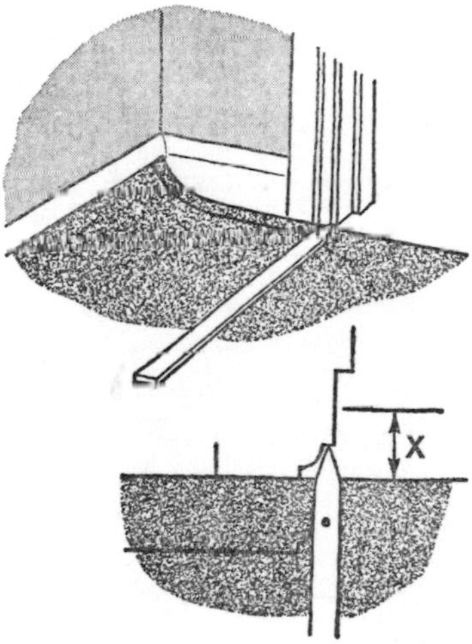

Fig. 23. Marking round door with scribing bar

Now the surplus at either end can be marked for trimming. Near to one end of the length, make a bold straight pencil mark that runs off the edge of the length on to the sub-floor. (See Fig. 24.) Adjust the cut end so that it rests closely against the skirting. Measure the distance between the mark on the sheet and the one on the sub-floor and re-set the nail on the scribing bar to this distance. (See Fig. 25.) Without disturbing the material, run the scribing bar along the end, keeping the bar at right angles to the skirting. The nail will score the

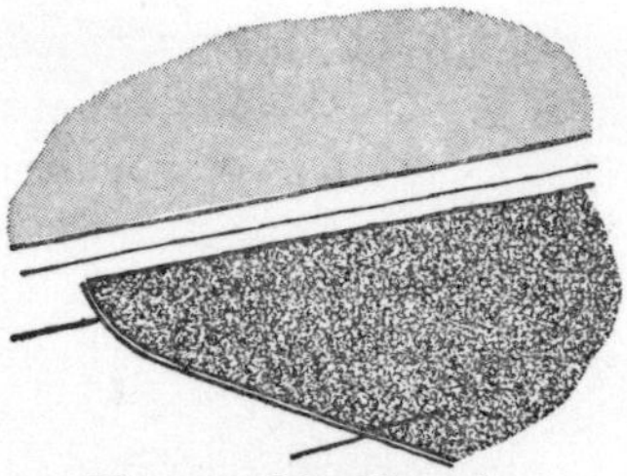

Fig. 24. Marking sheet flooring

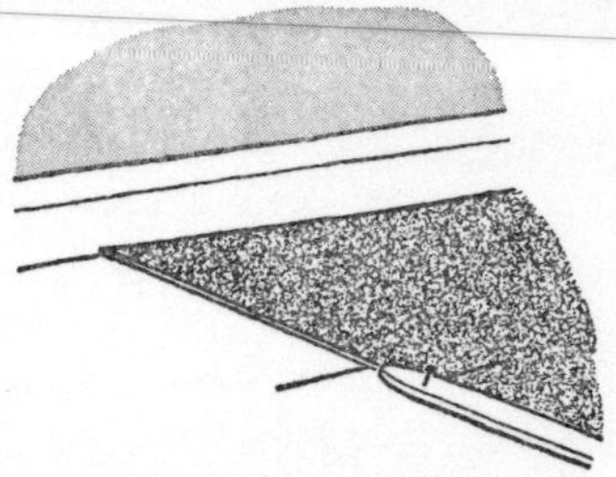

Fig. 25. Adjusting scribing bar

surface of the sheet, following faithfully any slope or hollow in the skirting. If you cut carefully to the scored line, that end of the sheet will make a perfect fit. Repeat the procedure at the other end, and with subsequent lengths.

The lengths should be laid with an overlap of about 1 in. at the joints, to allow for possible shrinkage. After about two weeks the joints can be trimmed-in. As the exposed overlap will be damaged, reverse the overlap to expose the clean edge and, with the aid of a long straightedge placed over the centre of the overlap, score through both thicknesses of the material. The edges can then be stuck down with a double-sided adhesive tape that is first stuck to the underlay while the edges of the material are held apart. They can then be pressed firmly back together and on to the tape.

When fitting the last length of material, or a piece into a window bay or recess, the floor will be covered so the guide marks for cutting of the surplus ends will have to be marked on the skirting. The trimming operation is just the same: Measure the gap between the lines when the material is pulled back, set this distance on the scribing bar, and score the guide line. Be sure to keep the bar at right angles to the skirting all the time.

To achieve a neat fit around w.c. and washbasin pedestals and similar obstructions, use some of the surplus paper felt to make a template, lay this at the appropriate point on the material and trace the outline for cutting.

Having cleaned the newly-laid tile or sheet floor with warm water containing a mild detergent (washing-up liquid) and used an abrasive powder on any really stubborn adhesive stains, go over the whole floor again with a damp mop, frequently wrung out in clean water. Never swill a new-laid floor with water; the adhesive takes at least five days to set fully. After that, apply two coats of a polish recommended by the flooring manufacturer, allowing the first coat to dry before applying the second. Despite the advertisements for 'miracle' polishes, their formula might be incompatible with a factory finish applied by the flooring manufacturer, so play safe. Thereafter, depending on the traffic, regular damp mopping, washing in hot water and mild detergent and an occasional coat of polish should be all that's needed.

LIQUID PLASTIC FLOORINGS

Another type of plastic flooring developed for and widely used in industrial and commercial applications has recently been packaged for the domestic market and is applied as you would apply paint. It provides a glossy, non-slip hardwearing covering, with no seams or cutting-in around doorways and other obstacles to worry about, and as it is sold in cans, you can bring it home in a shopping bag. Its decorative constituent consists of small plastic chippings and since these come in ten colours, that can be chosen and blended as you wish, the overall pattern and colour effect can be largely decided by you.

One such seamless floor sold in small kits suitable for domestic situations is Flecto, which can be applied over any clean, dry and level sub-floor. The kit has three components; a base coat, the coloured plastic chippings and a clear plastic top coat. The base coat, or sealer, is applied first. Normally, one coat will do, but if you are covering sheet lino or vinyl, two coats of a special sealer are recommended as a safeguard against the colours beneath bleeding through.

The base can be applied with a brush, but you would find it easier if you secured a paint roller to a broom handle and rolled it on. Once it is dry, apply a clear finishing coat, and while it is still tacky, sprinkle with coloured plastic chippings. It's best to work about 2 sq. yds. at a time, sprinkling the chippings over each freshly-spread area. When the whole floor is dry, sweep it over lightly with a clean stiff brush to remove any loose flakes of colour, and apply another coat of the clear finishing coat. When this has hardened, it should be sanded down all over with a medium-grade paper. This will slightly roughen the surface to make a good key for the third and final finishing coat.

A similar product that is aimed at the domestic market is Torginol Capri seamless flooring, which has a combined sealer and base coat.

THE CHOICE IN TIMBER

For the price of a cheap carpet, you can get a flooring that will last a lifetime in richly grained golden timber, and a flooring in which it is possible to 'weave' your own exclusive pattern. Wooden flooring is warm, comfortable and resilient underfoot and needs little maintenance, thanks to the latest types of finishes. You can choose from hardwearing Rhodesian teak, which will be completely unimpressed by stiletto heels, if they ever come back into fashion, mosaic squares incorporating light and dark woods, and many other attractive timbers, such as oak, maple and mahogany. The style is equally varied. There are individual strips about the size of a brick, small tiles consisting of a single sheet of plywood, and larger tiles made up into mosaics of multi-coloured timbers or one timber cut into many small strips and laid to a pattern on a backing sheet. Not so ornate, but most elegant are the strip floorings – narrow planks of varying lengths.

Strip flooring and tiles are the simplest forms to lay. The former are supplied in tongued and grooved planks $1\frac{3}{4}$ in. wide, $\frac{3}{8}$ in. thick and in random lengths from 18 in. to 7 ft. Short lengths are intermingled with long strips all over the floor and have to be 'secret nailed' to an existing timber floor. The first strip is laid with its tongue facing into the room and nailed through the tongue. The groove of the next strip is slipped over the tongue of the first, thus hiding the nails. Plain plywood tiles can be 6, 9 or 12 in. sq. and they are laid in either chequerboard or diamond patterns and are best laid so that the grain in each square runs at right angles to its neighbour. The laying of the larger tiles is in accordance with the pre-formed pattern.

If you are striving for a formal 'stately home' design of basket weave herringbone or brickbond parquet, you will have to use the bricksize blocks.

Tiles are generally fixed to their sub-floor with special adhesives. The small blocks can also be supplied for glueing, though there are types that are tongued and grooved for nailing to a timber sub-floor.

Most of the firms who supply these materials are geared to the needs of the do-it-yourself customer, and are quite accustomed to calculating his needs on the basis of a rough room plan containing the relevant dimensions. A new floor can thus be supplied as a kit containing all the necessary materials and laying instructions.

LAYING TIMBER FLOORINGS

When it comes to laying a timber floor, there are certain conditions that must be satisfied. As always, the sub-floor must be dry, clean and reasonably level. The last requirement is not as important for timber as it is for the other floor coverings discussed earlier, but the safest plan is to follow the manufacturer's advice. What *is* most important where timber floorings are concerned is the atmosphere. All timber contains an amount of moisture and your flooring will have been dried to a moisture content of around 12 per cent. If it is laid in an unused room in the damp of winter, it will probably absorb moisture, swell, and buckle. If you like to bask in oven temperatures, it could dry and shrink. Therefore, when it arrives, open the cartons and spread the material around so that it can adjust to the normal living temperature of the room, which means keeping it warm even though temporarily out of use. Ten days is not too long to let the timber get acclimatised. If you have underfloor central heating, specify kiln dried timber, and tell your supplier the reason because not all timbers are stable enough for these circumstances. If you have unwittingly chosen an unsuitable one (oak or mahogany, for example) he will probably be able to suggest a satisfactory alternative. These remarks apply mostly to natural timbers, as plywood floorings aren't affected to a great degree.

But, along with natural woodblock floors, they have to be given some room for expansion and contraction, and for this reason timber floors are never taken right up to the skirting boards. A gap of about ½ in. is recommended around all walls, which is filled with a cork strip on solid floors, and covered with timber beading nailed to the skirting on timber floors.

Some manufacturers supply floorings ready finished and no further treatment is necessary, save an occasional polishing. But most floorings are factory sanded and left unsealed, which is not a bad idea because you may find one or two noticeable projections when the floor is laid, which means a further sanding.

Using a machine sander is the only way to get a high quality finish and the drum sander as used by flooring contractors is the most efficient. These can be hired by the day, weekend or week in most areas, supplied with the necessary abrasive belts. A fine-grit belt should be sufficient for a new floor and when you are satisfied with the result, sweep the floor thoroughly as the machine's dustbag will not absorb all the fine particles.

You can protect your new floor either by traditional wax polishing or one of the tough polyurethane floor seals such as Bournseal or Ronseal Hardglaze. If you prefer a waxed finish, apply two coats of button polish first, to seal the pores of the timber against dirt. To apply polyurethane, rub a first coat well into the grain with a rag, then brush on at least two more coats, rubbing down lightly with fine glasspaper between coats.

FRESHENING OLD FLOORBOARDS

Don't overlook the possibility of creating, at next to no cost, a beautiful floor from the original floorboards. However rough and unattractive they may be now, it is possible that they could be transformed into a golden, grainy golden expanse you would be proud of. If you are not sure, carry out the following programme across a section of three or four boards to see how it looks before investing in a full-scale treatment.

Gaps must be filled. With big ones, wedge-shaped laths should be smeared with glue and tapped along the gap to a tight fit. When the glue has set, the surplus can be planed off. For small gaps, use a wood filler that matches as closely as possible the chosen fi ished colour of the boards. Nail heads must be punched below the surface and the holes filled with a matching filler. Renail all boards that have worked loose.

The next job is to sand the boards, using a powered drum

sander. If the boards are very bad, fit a coarse-grit sanding belt to the machine and work diagonally across the floor in one direction, then diagonally from the opposite direction, and finally along the grain. The boards should now be ready for sanding with a medium-grit belt (two or three treatments might be necessary) followed by a final smoothing with a fine-grit belt. When sanding, overlap each run by about 3 in. to avoid ridges.

The sanding machine will not be able to get into corners and probably not right up to the skirting boards. The easy way out would be to sand the perimeter boards as best you can by hand or by using a sanding disc in an electric drill, then stain the boards a dense dark colour that will mask the imperfections. If you want a finish that matches the rest, take the worst of the roughness off with an electric disc sander, but don't allow the edge of the disc to dig into the timber. Then use a good-quality, sharp handscraper and finish off with fine glasspaper.

The floor can now be stained, sealed and waxed or treated with three or four coats of polyurethane varnish. The points to watch when staining and polishing timber are covered in Chapter 7.

CERAMIC FLOOR TILES

One of the hardest wearing, easiest-to-clean floorings of all is ceramic tiles, as our Roman conquerors would realise, if they were around today to see the floors they laid 2,000 years ago. The best of tiles still come from Italy and Sicily in the most beautiful classical designs, but they are expensive – as much as £7 sq. yd. However, among the home produced ranges of mosaics, square, and hexagonal floor tiles, there are many attractive colours and patterns, and in the Chatsworth range from H. & R. Johnson, you can get patterned floor tiles that are also produced in a thinner matching range for applying to walls.

Ceramic tiles can be laid either in a thin bed of cement, or fixed to a prepared wooden sub-floor with special adhesive. As always, the sub-floor should be level, and free from damp, as described earlier.

The cement bed consists of 1 part cement to four parts of sharp sand, sparingly moistened with water. To test the consistency, tread in the mix; it should depress no more than about ½ in. under your weight and the pressure should not bring a watery film to the surface. Spread the mix about ½ in. thick with a rectangular float trowel – preferably a wooden one – and press the tiles in place, leaving a space of $\frac{1}{16}$th in. all round. Using a long board that is known to be true as a straightedge, and a spirit level, check that the tiles are flush and level, tapping down high spots, and adding a little more cement to low spots.

This is the tradesman's way, and a messy, laborious and difficult one it can be for the amateur, because great care is needed in getting a level surface. You would be more certain of avoiding bumps and hollows if you laid the tiles on a smooth hard foundation of chipboard.

Floorboards must be covered with ¾ in. chipboard, which should be screwed down rather than nailed, and sealed with two coats of polyurethane varnish. Set out a dry run of tiles, as described earlier and adjust until you have a minimum of half-a-tile width at the borders. They should be fixed with an adhesive recommended by the tile manufacturers. Leave for two or three days while the adhesive sets before grouting, a process described in Chapter 5. The technique of cutting the tiles is the same as that described for wall tiles in Chapter 5, with a slight variation to take account of the thicker, tougher material. When the cut has been made, lay the tile over a block of wood on a firm base with the waste portion just clear of the block's edge. Place another block of wood over the waste along the scribed line, and press down hard while supporting the wanted piece of tile. The tile will usually break clean, and any small uneven projections can be nibbled away with pincers, or smoothed down with carborundum stone.

Chapter 7: DECORATIVE TREATMENTS FOR FURNITURE

Though built-in cupboards in kitchens and bathrooms will usually be redecorated with the rest of the room, as part of the woodwork, there will be occasions when other types of furniture will be badly in need of a face lift, if it is not to let down the rest of the decoration scheme. The paint on the chests of drawers and the like will chip and fade, just like the rest of the woodwork; polished furniture, coffee table tops and so on will become stained and dull over the years, despite religious polishing. There are many kinds of finish that can be applied to furniture, though they fall into two basic categories – painting, and staining and polishing. The preparation for painting is much the same as already described in Chapter 2, and of course the same kind of paints that are suitable for the woodwork of the room will be entirely satisfactory when applied to furniture. But to refurbish furniture with a natural finish requires quite different techniques.

Most old pieces will have been varnished in their natural state, or stained first and then varnished, and this old finish should be entirely removed, if it is in bad condition. Total stripping to remove white rings and cigarette burns may not be necessary, and we will see how such repairs can be done later in this chapter.

Stripping old varnish is a messy operation, but not difficult. Choose a warm dry day, if you can, and take the piece of furniture into the garden to work on. You will need some rags, a basin, a roll of fine steel wool and a bottle of solvent to dissolve the finish. Which solvent you use will depend on the type of finish applied to the furniture. In most cases, white spirits or methylated spirits will work; if they don't, the surface may have been sprayed with a cellulose varnish, and cellulose thinners will therefore be required. One or the other will dissolve the varnish. Apply plenty of solvent from the basin, and scrub at the surface with pads of coarse steel wool, squeezing the scrubbed-up varnish out of the steel wool pad into an old tin as you go. When you come to the legs, stand each one in the basin of solvent so that the solvent dribbles back for re-use. A nail brush will be extremely useful for working solvent into carvings in the legs and any deep gouges elsewhere. When most of the mess has been removed, clean up the piece of furniture with fresh solvent and clean rags.

Once back to the bare wood, there are several courses open to you. If the colour of the wood is too light, you can stain it darker; if it is too dark, you can bleach it lighter and then apply either a clear varnish or a modern stain in one of the gay colours that have become fashionable in recent years. However, achieving the desired result can be something of a trial and error process, so if possible, experiment on the inner surface of a door or other area that is not going to show.

We will look at each of these treatments in more detail in a moment, but whichever of them you choose, painstaking preparation of the bare wood is vital to a good quality finish, since blemishes will not merely show through the transparent film of varnish – they will be heightened by it. The surface should be well sanded with flour glasspaper or 280 grade wet-or-dry. Always work along the grain and be particularly careful in corners to avoid using the paper with a circular motion. Never use a disc sander in an electric drill for this purpose, and if you use a finishing sander drill attachment, give the surfaces a final rub down by hand to remove the minute 'fish scale' abrasions the sander will leave behind.

If you want a glass-smooth finish, the grain will probably have to be filled, or you will have to build up coat after coat of finish. There are several fillers designed for the purpose, obtainable from decorator's shops, but as it's easy to make a mess of the surface, you ought to practice first on a spare piece of wood. When the surface has been sanded as smooth as you can get it, dust it off and apply the filler with a coarse rag or clean sacking, rubbing it hard across the grain. Most grain fillers are pastes that have to be thinned to a creamy consistency with white spirit, and it is crucial that the surplus is removed from the surface before the paste sets. This is where difficulties might arise: In wiping the surface clean, care has to be taken not to remove the filler from the pores of the wood, which merely puts you back where you started, or, in striving to avoid this, leaving too much paste behind, resulting in a smeary surface.

Grain fillers can be obtained in most natural wood tones, and if you intend staining a surface, an oil-based filler could be mixed with one of the naphtha stains, such as those made by Colron and Rustins, thus ensuring that the filler is an exact match for your finish. Fillers are indispensable for obliterating burns and deep scores, but it's a matter of personal choice whether one uses them extensively. Really old pieces of furniture that have been knocked about over the years, such as blanket chests and settles, might lose a lot of their character if restored to a new condition. Also, the generally accepted furniture finish today is a matt satin one in which there has been no attempt to fill in the texture of the grain in pursuit of a mirror-like gloss.

If you want to lighten the colour of the wood before refinishing or there are disfiguring stains here and there on the surface, you will have to bleach the whole piece. Oxalic acid, which can be bought from the chemist, is a good, cheap bleaching agent. Use about one tablespoonful to a pint of water. Much more effective, however, is Rustins Super Wood Bleach, a two part treatment in which a solution is brushed on and, ten minutes later, neutralised by a second solution.

Of the many finishing treatments you can choose from, an oiled finish is the easiest and quickest to achieve. Any of the proprietary teak oils found in decorator's shops will do, but neat boiled linseed oil will not produce a satisfactory result; it tends to remain gummy and will attract dirt. Teak oil should be applied liberally with a rag, left to soak in for a few minutes and then the surplus removed with a clean dry rag. Leave the piece to dry for about six hours and repeat the process. Three or four such applications might be needed on new work, but thereafter a twice-yearly treatment should be sufficient. Destroy all rags immediately after use as in drying out they could catch fire through spontaneous combustion.

A natural step from an oiled finish is wax polish, which

results in a better sheen than can be achieved with oil, though it involves much more work in keeping a pristine appearance. The bare surface should first be sealed (after staining, where applicable) with two coats of clear button polish. Rub the first one well into the surface with a rag, brush the second coat on quickly and rub it down lightly with fine steel wool when dry. This foundation is necessary to prevent dirt from percolating through a soft film of wax and into the wood, where a permanent grey bloom would result.

The alternative finishes are a stain followed by clear varnish or a combined stain and varnish. The latter method is not always satisfactory for a number of reasons. Several coats may be needed to produce a desirable surface, with the probable consequence that you get a darker finish than you had intended. A single coat could produce the right colour but a weak film, and if this is scratched or scuffed, the colour of the bare wood might show through.

Clear varnish treatments can be applied to all woods, from pale white birch to ruddy mahogany. They will darken the surface slightly, but, as explained, this could be counteracted by first bleaching the wood. Traditional varnishes are best left to the craftsman because there are so many types and colours for all sorts of situations that they lead to needless complications for the amateur.

Stick, therefore, to the modern polyurethanes which are easy to apply and give a very durable finish in a choice of high gloss, satin or matt sheen. However, some brands are tougher than others, and generally it pays to buy the dearer ones, as these are likely to have a greater proportion of the all-important polyurethane in their formulation. The three main types are called two-pack, moisture-cured and air drying. Two-pack formulations are mostly used in industry and also favoured by keen yachtsmen. They are not easy to apply, and not really necessary for domestic situations. Moisture-cured polyurethanes also have high resistance to wear, but are slow to use; drying time between coats is about 12 hours and could be longer in conditions of high humidity. The most widely available for domestic use are the air drying type, under such brand names as Ronseal and Furniglas. Drying time is up to 1½ hours and they give a harder film than conventional varnishes. Use a good quality brush, and flow the varnish on with a minimum of brushing, allowing the varnish to level out itself. On vertical surfaces, some care must be taken not to be over-liberal in application, but you will not find it difficult to strike a balance between too much and too little. At least two coats will be needed and each coat should be rubbed down with fine glasspaper or steel wool used lightly along the grain. If a gloss polyurethane is used, the more coats applied, the higher the gloss achieved, and it is possible to reach a finish closely resembling that of high gloss french polishing.

Stains, or wood dyes as they are sometimes called, are available in many timber colours, from light oak to rosewood. They consist of finely ground pigments in a water, spirit or oil base, and Furniglas produce a range said to be fadeless that is dispersed in a combination of water and alcohol. Water and spirit-based stains tend to fade under prolonged exposure to sunlight and a hardwearing bond between oil and oil-based stain and varnish finish can be difficult to achieve. Water-based stains will cause the surface grain of the wood to swell, roughening the surface, so before the final sanding, rub a well-damped – but not saturated – cloth over the area to raise the grain. Even when this roughness has been cut back, application of the stain might still produce a detectable roughness, if the wood is very porous, and a further light sanding could be necessary followed by another coat of stain. For this reason, it is often worthwhile diluting the first coat of stain, so that too great a depth of colour is not produced. Stains are best applied with a rag. When a brush is used, there is a risk of dark blotches resulting from the concentration of stain where the bristles first touch the wood. After staining, leave the piece two or three hours to dry. If the grain has been filled, leave it overnight. When dry, the stained surfaces can be varnished or waxed.

Another kind of finish that has recently become popular is the coloured polyurethane stain. The colours are always bold – scarlet, turquoise, gold and so on – and combine the liveliness of colour with the natural appearance of the wood because they allow the grain and texture to be seen. Usually, they are both a stain and a varnish, so the earlier remarks about the darkening effect on the wood apply. One coat or two will be sufficient when protected by a coat of clear polyurethane. Proprietary makes of these finishes readily available are marketed by Blackfriar, A. Sanderson (Translac) and Ronseal. To see the kind of effect they produce, look in the furniture departments of the more go-ahead stores and the adventurous small shops that are usually described as boutiques.

For a stain and varnish finish to be effective, the bare wood must obviously possess a grain that has eye appeal. Hardwoods will not be lacking in this, but only the lighter ones, such as oak and beech, lend themselves to staining in bold colours. With the major exception of red cedar, most softwoods – red and yellow pine, spruce and birch – are suitable for colouring, though the grain may not be prominent. A great deal of plywood furniture, for example, has insufficient character for a natural finish and looks best when painted. This is particularly true of the cheap whitewood units, sold mainly for kitchens and bedrooms. To keep the price down, these are generally made from a birch plywood which has few knots and a faint grain like watered silk, but since such furniture is made to be painted, no trouble is taken to match the veneers in manufacture and knot holes are filled with elliptical plugs of veneer. Obviously, there is no natural beauty to be revealed here. However, Finnish birch plywood comes in several grades and a B grade or B/BB grade can be stained and varnished with rewarding results. The B grade is the operative one because the veneer is selected for its grain and knots and adjoining veneers are matched for colour. The B/BB grade has B quality on one side, and BB quality – suitable only for painting – on the other.

An old-fashioned finish that is again beginning to find favour is ebonising – a dense, matt black finish that still allows the grain to show through, if not overdone. There are several 'ebony' or black oak stains on the market and one of these should be applied to the surface and treated when dry with one or two coats of a matt polyurethane varnish.

The other traditional natural finish is french polish. French polish is made from shellac dissolved in alcohol and applied by a special technique that takes a lot of practice to perfect and is, to the inexperienced, somewhat tiring to use. The amateur, would probably be better served by one of the treatments mentioned earlier when completely renovating a piece of furniture. However, french polishing is an ideal way to restore damaged areas on otherwise respectable pieces of furniture that are already french polished, or have a modern, factory applied cellulose finish, such as TV sets and radiograms.

The damaged portion must be smoothed with fine abrasive as described and then wiped over with white spirit. Apply the first coat of french polish with a soft brush evenly and quickly and allow to dry. If the polish raises some of the grain, lightly glasspaper again until it is smooth, and apply a second coat in the same way. A finish to match the rest of the surface is built up from subsequent coats of french polish applied with the craftsman's 'rubber'. To make this, place a wad of cotton wool on a piece of clean white linen or cotton sheet about the size of a handkerchief. Saturate the cotton wool, with polish and wrap the rag around it, twisting the ends together. This is your rubber. Press it on an old piece of wood to remove the surface polish, then work the rubber over the area to be treated in circular or figure-of-eight movements. Never let it come to rest, as this will cause it to stick to the surface, producing an unsightly patch which will have to be erased and repolished. As the polish in the cotton wad is used up, apply more pressure to force more polish through the rag.

Allow the surface to dry for a few minutes before applying another coat and carry on in this manner until you have a surface that matches the rest. As a finishing touch, thin the remaining polish in the rubber with methylated spirits and squeeze almost dry, then work the rubber in even strokes, backwards and forwards over the area. This is the basic technique of french polishing, and the same procedure would be used for the complete refinishing of a piece of furniture. When working large areas, it would be advisable to dab a small quantity of linseed oil on the surface of the rubber to act as a lubricant.

A product specially developed for the unskilled to use is Furniglas Home French Polish, which can be used to repair surface blemishes without completely stripping the original finish or as a finish for new or stripped furniture. With this, a basic polish is applied with a pad, then burnished with a second liquid, applied with cotton wool and dried off with a duster to produce a deep gloss.

Deep scores in a wooden surface can often be successfully

camouflaged quite simply. If the surface has been waxed polished, it should first be cleaned with white spirit. A shellac varnish stain of the appropriate shade should be applied to the crack with an artists' brush in as many coats as it takes to fill the score until slightly proud of the surface. Allow each coat to dry before applying the next, and smooth the final coat flush with the surface, using fine abrasive paper as described. To bring the gloss back, apply a proprietary polish reviver or metal polish. The surface can then be re-waxed or varnished. Children's wax crayons and even shoe polish can be used as fillers, if blended to match the colour of the wood.

Melt wax crayon, fill the depression with it, and when it has hardened, scrape off the excess flush with the surface. The wax must be coated with button polish before any other finish can be applied, and of course the wax could break down if subjected to heat. Cigarette burns can be treated in the same way, once all charred wood has been scraped away.

If a depression is a small one, you might be able to swell the wood fibres and thus remove the worst of the damage, ready for repolishing or varnishing. Soak a tea cloth in water, wring out the surplus and fold the cloth in several thicknesses. Then place it over the depression and press a hot iron on it. The steam created will raise the fibres, though you might have to repeat the operation several times to get a satisfactory result. When you have, smooth the surface with glasspaper and touch up the area with polish or varnish.

Although we suggest, in the interests of saving you work, that repaired patches should be touched up to match the existing surface finish, this will not always work, as under the reflection of light, the new patch might show. If this is noticeable enough to bother you, the only course is to remove the existing finish and retreat the whole surface. Or to paint it, which brings us to our final treatment for furniture.

The preparation programme described in Chapter 2 is additionally important with furniture. You can, to some extent, get away with uneven work on window frames and skirting boards because they are not there to be noticed. But furniture is, so resolve from the start to take extra care. Spend extra time in sanding the wood and rubbing down cracks after filling to remove all traces of surplus. Remove all handles and other protrusions before you start. Before the final sanding down, wipe all surfaces over with a damp cloth to raise the grain; then you can be sure of a satin-smooth foundation. Work the priming paint well into the surface and lay off in one direction, lightly with the brush tip. Primers tend to show brush marks which will have to be removed if they are not to show through the undercoat.

Furniture has lots more corners and edges than most other subjects for painting and more attention is needed here to achieve a crisp, smooth finish. Never paint inwards from an edge, as this will produce an unsightly thick build-up along the edge and probably tear marks on the adjacent surface as well. If it does happen, wipe off the affected part while wet with white spirits and start again, or rub down and repaint if it has dried.

Work, if you can, in a room with a gentle background warmth; garages and sheds tend to be dusty always, and they can be cold and damp – conditions that could spoil your work or slow up the drying. If you stand the piece of work on battens on clean sheets of newspaper, painting around the base will be easier and there will be no danger of picking up dust on your brush. To paint chair or table legs, insert wood screws into the feet to raise them off the floor. The sequence for painting such furniture is to turn it upside down, painting the legs, rungs and undersides first. A chair can be rested by its seat on a table while this is done. Remove sliding doors from their tracks and mask the top and bottom edges as paint here could cause the doors to stick in their tracks. Raise them from table or floor for painting by resting them on battens.

As a precaution against warping, drawers fronts and doors should be painted on both sides, so that moisture in the air cannot be absorbed from one side. This is particularly important with sliding doors and kitchen and bathroom furniture. If possible, paint the backs of kitchen and bathroom units as well, to protect them from condensation. Leave the paint to harden for two or three days preferably in a warm room, before refixing handles and other items.

Furniture that is fit only for painting need not be refurbished exclusively with paint. You could veneer it, or parts of it, or you could apply other decorative materials – plastic laminate, hessian, self-adhesive plastics such as Fablon, and even wallpaper. In the fabric departments of many big stores and do-it-yourself shops you can find upholstery-quality sheet vinyls with a rich leather look which can also be used to lift a piece of furniture out of the junk category into the role of a prestige drawing-room piece. Humble whitewoods can be given charm and gaiety with applied decoration in the form of coloured stick-on motifs and ornamental mouldings in classical forms – scrolls, tassels, Grecian urns, etc.

Here are a few ideas for such treatments to start you off thinking up your own:

Paper the panels of a wardrobe door with the bedroom wallpaper. A coat of transparent wallpaper protector such as Fend will prolong its life. Paint the rest of the piece white.

Cover a dressing table top with a plastic laminate and apply an edging trim of timber or plastic. Timber yards or do-it-yourself shops are bound to stock one or more of the products produced exactly for this purpose. Veneer a battered old coffee table with a fool-proof product such as Handi-veneer. This incorporates its own adhesive which is activated by the heat from an electric iron. Teak, mahogany and oak veneers are available, and there are matching edging veneers for materials up to $\frac{3}{4}$ in. thick.

Cover the drawer fronts of an old chest with a sumptuous, leather-look vinyl or hessian. Panel a dull bedhead with one of the quilted and buttoned vinyls – a luxury touch that could be carried through on wardrobe door panels and the room door itself. Reproduction antique knobs and handles in brass, wrought iron and other finishes are not hard to find and these alone could inexpensively transform a beat-up old wreck, once varnishing or repainting has been completed.

Chapter 8: BEGINNER'S GUIDE TO INTERIOR DESIGN

There is really no mystique about interior decoration, though you could be forgiven for thinking there is, on reading some of the pompous articles and explanatory captions to pictures that appear in many of the glossy home magazines. There is a basic discipline, and there are some basic rules, but they are few and simple and never absolute. They can be bent or broken pretty well whenever it pleases you – but know what they are so that, if you decide to ride roughshod over them, you at least know what you could be letting yourself in for. The components of any decorative scheme are Colour, Pattern and Texture, and as colour is the universal one, let's consider that first.

Colours can be classified as warm or cool. Scientifically, black and white are not colours, though for our purposes, they can be described as neutral colours that will blend with virtually all the others. The six basic colours are those seen in a rainbow – yellow, orange, red (the warm colours) and violet, blue, green (the cool colours). They are not, of course, clear-cut and just as they shade into each other, in a rainbow, so the intermixing of paint or dye pigments produces an infinite variety of shades. All we need concern ourselves with is the warm or cool effects that they produce when used in decoration.

In our mainly tepid climate, it would be sensible to choose colour schemes dominated by the warm end of the spectrum for dull rooms on the shady or North side of a house which gets no direct sun, and for bedrooms and bathrooms where the illusion of warmth is worth fostering. But there is no reason at all why they should be reserved for such situations, and it would equally be wrong to suggest that rooms facing South should necessarily be decorated in cool colours. Apply British commonsense and compromise, therefore, in selecting colour for British temperatures.

The other basic rule about colour is that pale colours recede and bold colours advance. Not literally, of course, but this is the effect they have on the eye. Thus, pastel and pale tints will make a room look larger, and bright, strong colours will, by arresting the eye, make a door or wall seem nearer than it is. Pale colours also reflect more light than intense colours. Therefore, in a small or dark room, consider carefully before making a bold splash. It might not matter, but it could, and only the trial-and-error approach will resolve the problem for you.

Pattern will inevitably come into your scheme. Even if all the fabrics in a room – curtains, upholstery, carpets – and the walls are plain colours, pattern will be introduced by the furniture itself in the arrangement of chairs, the grain of a wooden table, of pictures on the wall, well-stocked bookshelves, lighting fittings and so on. These will all add varied shapes and colours, and thus make patterns. But when most of us think of pattern, we think of it as applied to fabrics, floorings and wall coverings and this kind of pattern cannot be considered in a vacuum. Colour is an integral part of it, and the earlier remarks about colour must be borne in mind when selecting patterns.

It is in selecting pattern that the most discipline is needed. Generally, it is wiser to stick to one bold pattern only, and certainly be very wary about introducing secondary patterns. If, for example, you have a carpet with a heavy floral design, keep to a light geometric pattern or pale stripe for wallpaper or curtains. Upholstered furniture in a bold design could be teamed with a modest wallpaper or curtain pattern, but not with heavily patterned carpet.

The aim should always be to strike a balance between what is stimulating and what is restful, and the eye and the mind will quickly tire of too much stimulation. Don't forget that the rest of the furnishings – natural timber furniture, china, ornaments, pictures, etc. – are going to contribute their visual quota to the finished effect.

Where does a good decoration scheme start? More often than not, it will have to be planned around a major item of furniture such as a good carpet or lounge suite. If the item has a bold pattern, let it be the dominant note in the room. One approach is to analyse the colours it contains and base the overall new colour scheme on its principle colour. You are not likely to have bought it if it didn't contain your favourite colour, and you could match it or introduce a variation in tone on the walls. Alternatively a gay contrasting colour could be used to give a new punch to the familiar, old one, and supported with a third containing echoes of the original. Let's say you have a three-piece suite, heavily patterned with pink roses on a charcoal background. This could be teamed with a pale plain grey, carpet, and a grey/pink patterned paper, or three walls with a Regency striped grey paper and one painted a deep, dramatic colour – a deep bluish purple, say. The curtains could then pick up the pink theme or the purple.

Note that this scheme uses only three basic colours, which is always a sound principle. Too many colours, like too many patterns, would soon become an irritant, and the rest of the colour and pattern interest should be left to casual furniture, cushions, table lamps and so on.

On those fortunate occasions you can start from scratch, and perhaps thereby make good earlier mistakes, it would be no bad idea to emulate the restrained approach of architects and trained designers to the main shell of the room. Their preference is usually to treat the walls just as a backcloth and let the furniture and accessories take the stage. White painted walls are the perfect foil for favourite prints, plaques and other wall hangings. They will also set off to advantage any kind of polished wood furniture, and upholstery. This treatment also has the advantage that you could paint one wall any traffic-stopping colour you like. If it doesn't work (and it probably will) you could change it in an afternoon for just a few shillings.

While the austere treatment of the basic shell by the professional is excellent for communal rooms, a more orthodox treatment would probably be more satisfying for bedrooms. The main guideline here is: Keep it restful. Choose warm colours in the paler tints for the main background, but don't be afraid of dropping in explosive little punches of colour in the form of bedspreads and other accessories. Likewise, kitchens should be cheerful but restful. Avoid jazzy patterns on floors and worktops and remember that a lot of the kitchen equipment will add colour, shape and interest to the finished scheme.

To a large extent, the question of texture will look after itself, because the component materials in any room will range from smooth, hard timber to soft upholstery and thick-piled rugs or carpets. But don't ignore the dramatic contrasts that can be produced by careful use of textures. Think, for instance, of a stone fireplace offset by a timber wall; a shaggy rug on a polished timber floor; a silky wallpaper and a candlewick bedspread.

The same sort of care that goes into choosing a colour scheme should be given to the layout of a room. Too often, pieces of furniture are simply strung out along the walls and a U-shape created around the hearth with a three-piece suite. Napoleon didn't manage to break the British Square at Waterloo, but it's time you did! Again, there can be no absolute rules when considering furniture arrangement, but the effect to aim for would be the creation of two, or possibly more, groupings so that there is more than one centre of interest in a room. In a sitting room one of them will obviously home on the hearth, or, in a home with central heating, perhaps on the television set. Bookshelves and a writing desk or display shelves and an occasional table could be grouped to provide other focal points. In a through room which has to include dining room furniture, the sideboard could perhaps be placed at right-angles to a wall to act as a room divider between the lounging and eating areas. Paint, wallpaper or open shelving would disguise the unattractive back. Though not much can be done with the average bedroom, the grouping of wardrobes and chests of drawers can be better than placing them equally around the perimeter. Experiment by drawing a room plan to scale on graph paper, cut pieces of coloured paper to scale in the shape of furniture pieces, and shuffle them around on the plan to find a suitable layout.

The same approach can be used successfully with the accessories that will put the finishing touches to your completed scheme. A series of small pictures will look better when massed on one section of wall – say the chimney breast – than dissipated over a wide area. On display units, arrange your favourite pieces in clusters punctuated by spaces, rather than spreading them out uniformly to fill the shelves. Treat the books on bookshelves the same way.

The scheme that throbs with life by day can be killed stone dead the moment you switch on the light. More often than not, the death ray is a pendant fitting dangling from the centre of the room. Like colour and pattern, lighting must be balanced to provide a soft, overall distribution of light, and functional light as needed at individual points for reading, sewing, writing, etc. It should also be flexible enough to give a restful background light for listening to music and watching TV. One central pendant can never provide all this, so it will have to be supplemented with wall brackets, table lamps, and/or floor standard lamps. In fact, with this kind of combination, you will probably never use the central pendant again.

Unless you are deliberately striving for a 'mood' effect, avoid opaque shades which will throw the light directly upwards and downwards, creating hard shadows. Translucent shades will give a better, diffused light. And don't be stingy with the size of bulb you choose; a 100-watt bulb will burn for 10 hours for less than 2d. For general lighting, a central pendant should be fitted with a 150 or 200-watt bulb. Fit 100-watt bulbs in table lamps and 100 or 150-watt bulbs in standard lamps. For wall brackets, choose 60 or 75-watt bulbs. If a conventional lamp is too big to fit in a lighting fitting, be careful about using one of the high-output, mushroom shaped lamps. Fittings bought from reputable stores are these days usually sold bearing a recommendation on the size of lamp to fit.

Chapter 9: HOW TO TACKLE EXTERIOR PAINTING

If, in this capricious climate of ours, there can be a best time to tackle outside painting, it is towards the end of September. Spring is usually unsettled, showers can ruin newly-applied paint, and damp patches of wood should be given all the time possible to dry out. Hot midsummer sunshine can make paint difficult to apply and unnaturally speeds the drying. So we come to the early Autumn, when the weather is supposed to be most settled and when the sunshine will be kind, allowing the paint to cure naturally in time for winter's worst, and the ravages of the next five years or so.

Apart from the season, the other best time to start is just before you really need to. If you catch the finish before it begins noticeably to crack up, you will be involved in a lot less preparatory labour.

Painting the outside is much the same as painting the inside, but painstaking preparation and a methodical approach are even more essential: The risk of deterioration in exposed conditions is greater, and the consequences of slap-happy workmanship more difficult to put right. Let's assume the worst possible case: A neglected house with four or five colours in various stages of peeling back to the bare wood, rusting metalwork, and wall rendering that is crumbling in places and covered with some form of flaking colour. If you were stout hearted enough to take on the whole task in one exhausting session, the sequence of working would be gutters, walls, pipes and woodwork. But you probably aren't, so we will take the logical division: Woodwork, guttering, etc., then rendered walls. Start with the gutters, scooping out any accumulation of silt and leaves, wipe clean and coat the inside only with a bitumenous paint. Examine gutter brackets and renew any weakened by rust. Paintwork in good condition on the guttering exterior can be rubbed down with a middle grade abrasive paper ready for undercoat and gloss. If the guttering is in bad condition use a metal scraper to remove as much paint as you can. Rust should be abraded to a fairly bright finish and such patches treated immediately, before a damp atmosphere can cause further oxidisation. There are many makes of metal primer, rich in zinc to provide a form of galvanisation, and other types called rust inhibitors. These combine chemically with any ingrained rust to provide a firm base for finishing paint, and there is less chance of future breakdown with these on an inadequately prepared surface.

If the woodwork of fascia boards, window frames and doors has to be stripped bare, your best tool is a blowlamp: chemical stripping is slow and expensive for such large areas. Burners attached to disposable butane gas cartridges are the handiest, though the long-established paraffin lamp is more economical, but whichever you use, there are safety precautions you must observe. Always be aware of the direction in which the flame is pointing, and that should always be away from you and any glass. With an absent-minded turn of the wrist it could catch your clothing or exposed hand, and while these are unpleasant enough in themselves, their consequences would be more serious if they resulted in you falling off the ladder. For the same reasons, keep your hands out of the way of the charred paint, as it falls away under the scraper. Take care when putting the lamp down for a moment there is nothing combustible near the flame. Never use a blowlamp on or near the eaves, as the current of air passing through here could carry sparks into the roof space, which could cause a fire. Rely in these situations on hand scrapers or chemical strippers. If you are working around open windows, take down curtains first. To avoid charring the wood, the lamp must be kept moving. Immediately you see the paint blister fully, simultaneously direct the flame at the next patch while removing the already softened paint with the scraper. Try to keep going in one steady movement. Use a chemical stripper or a hand scraper on window frames where they meet the glass, which would crack under the flame's heat.

Bare woodwork should be primed soon after to seal out the damp, so when burning off, plan the work so that before you finish for the day, all stripped surfaces have been primed, and resinous knots treated beforehand, as described in Chapter 2. The priming paint should be worked well into any cracks, before they are filled. Use an exterior grade stopper for filling and pack it down tightly. Pay particular attention to the joints in window frames, because this is one of the first places where a coat of paint fails, due to the expansion and contraction of the timber.

Priming paint can be left uncovered for a week or more without coming to any harm, but you should strive to get undercoat covered by its protective top coat of gloss as quickly as possible.

Paint work in reasonably sound condition should be washed down with a solution of detergent, to remove atmospheric dirt and grease, then rinsed and dried. Follow up with a thorough rub-down with medium grade glasspaper to remove the gloss and provide a key for the ensuing coat. The prescribed paint programme is: One primer, worked well into the grain; one undercoat and two top coats with a light rub-down using fine glasspaper between each. For exterior work, however, a third top coat is a good investment. Again, a light rub-down with fine glasspaper should precede the final coat. After each rub-down, wipe the treated woodwork over with a clean rag moistened, not saturated, in white spirits immediately prior to painting.

The techniques of applying paint and cutting-in round window panes are described in Chapter 3 but there are other points to be watched when painting the outside. In the openings for hinged windows you will find a lot of fiddly rebates and there will be a temptation to daub the paint on, as it will never come under close scrutiny. Be firm: over-thick coats will prevent the windows from closing properly. If the paint is also applied carelessly, it could soon crack in the angles of the rebates and gradually flake. The same precautions should be taken when painting the edges of opening windows, and when tackling these, don't forget the top and bottom edges.

Obviously, you wouldn't carry on painting when it is raining, but in your eagerness to get the job done, you could start too early and carry on too long and thus find that the dew has spoiled some of your work. To avoid the first mistake, follow the sun when painting. As it moves around, it will evaporate the dew. To avoid the second, stop work well before the shadows begin to lengthen. Never paint with a hot sun directly on your back. Apart from harmfully accelerating the drying process, it could draw from the wood moisture that would otherwise lie dormant, but in the circumstances, produce a damp patch that will cause the paint to blister.

'Be systematic,' we said at the beginning of this chapter, and the following break-down of the ideal work sequence will be of help to you in pursuit of this aim. But of far more help will be your commonsense and estimated rate of progress (no cheating, now!) in relation to the size of your house. When you have completed items 1 to 5 below, you will have a reasonable idea of how you are getting along. After that, it might be more sensible to work just one, or perhaps two, sides of the house at a time, bearing in mind that it is desirable to get one top coat over the undercoat as soon as you can. If at any time you get caught between stages while waiting for one coat to dry, you could perhaps prepare and prime a door. Or have an early night.

1. Clean out and repair guttering as necessary. Paint the insides.
2. Prepare outer surfaces of guttering, piping, etc. Prime bare metal.
3. Prepare and prime where necessary facia boards and soffits behind guttering.
4. Prepare and prime upper floor windows, including the renewal of loose patches of putty and the easement of sticking windows and hinges.
5. Undercoat on guttering, piping, facia boards, soffits and upper floor windows.
6. Prepare and prime ground floor windows.
7. First top coat on gutters, etc., and upper windows.
8. Undercoat on ground floor windows.
9. Second top coat on guttering, etc., and upper floor windows.
10. First top coat on ground floor windows.
11. Prepare and prime doors.
12. Second top coat on ground floor windows.
13. Complete doors, alternating with third top coat, if desired.

HANDLING A LADDER

While all this has been going on, you will have been wrestling with a fairly heavy and ungainly extension ladder for a great part of the time. And all-too-often, the novice wastes a lot of energy in the process, and risks injury, so here are some tips on how to handle it with safety. To carry it from place to place, keep it upright in its shortest position and held firmly against one hip. If it is resting against the eaves, you can roll or slide it along. To extend the ladder, brace it between the knees and check that it is clear of telephone wires, trees, or other projections and lift it a few rungs at a time. Rest it on a convenient rung while changing grip, and if it has to be extended higher than you can comfortably reach, lay it on the ground to do so. To get it upright again, place the foot of the ladder against the wall, lift it by the top rung as high as you can, and as soon as you can get underneath it, 'walk' it upright, pushing on the rungs hand-over-hand.

The correct angle at which to use a ladder is one foot out from the wall for every four feet up. If there is no one that can steady the ladder for you by standing on the bottom rung when it is resting on hard smooth surfaces, place a sack or a sheet of rough material under the ladder's feet. If in doubt, secure it with lashings to stakes driven into the ground (See Fig. 26), or use longer rope to secure it around the frames of open windows. If you have to pack under the feet on an uneven hard surface, use good-size thick boards as thin, small scraps could split or slip out of place. On soft earth, set the ladder in position, then jump on the bottom rung to settle the ladder firmly.

To reach guttering height safely, you should extend the ladder two or three rungs beyond the guttering. Handle the ladder very carefully when resting it against guttering – particularly if it's made of vinyl, where the weight could force the guttering out of its supporting brackets. There are splayed-arm braces that can be fitted to keep the top of the ladder away from the wall in such circumstances. Work within a comfortable arm's reach; overstretching can result in overbalancing.

To keep both hands as free as possible for working, a short apron with pockets is an invaluable place to store rags, scrapers and similar tools. The paint kettle should be suspended by a

Fig. 26. Methods of lashing a ladder

hook from a convenient rung of the ladder. When climbing or descending, have at least one hand firmly gripping a stile, sliding it along as you progress. If both hands are free, grip the rungs. Finally, wear thick-soled shoes – they will reduce foot-fatigue.

If you are nervous at the prospect of using a ladder, you might consider one of the lightweight, clip-together scaffold tower kits that are available. They are fairly expensive to buy, but in most big towns there are plant hire firms who would rent one to you by the day, weekend, or week. They come in a choice of heights terminating in a stout wooden platform from which to work. A scaffold tower is certainly a better operational base when it comes to tackling the high sections of walls. Cement paints and the like are heavy to handle in buckets, and a small paint kettle is not a very practical vessel for the large quantities to be handled. This could also apply to such preparatory tasks as hacking out and renewing loose patches of rendering, where heavy bucketsful of concrete will be used.

PAINTING WALLS

If the walls of your house are of brick, think carefully before deciding to paint them, because you will merely be creating additional hard work for yourself in maintaining their attractive appearance. If the brickwork is porous, better to apply a clear silicone water repellant which is invisible and cannot therefore look unsightly, as a deteriorating painted surface will.

Rendered surfaces generally look better for a paint treatment, but first they must be thoroughly prepared. Hair cracks in an otherwise smooth, sound surface will be obliterated by the paint, but noticeable cracks should be filled. First open them out with an old screwdriver, trowel, or similar tool, raking the crack to a wedge shape that is narrowest at the surface. This affords a good key for the pointing material. Don't use a hammer and chisel to widen the crack, because the shock could cause further fractures. Try suspect patches for soundness by tapping lightly with the shaft of the hammer, and listening for a hollow note. Loose portions must be chipped back to where the rendering is bonded firmly, and a little beyond, just to be sure.

The mix for the new patch of rendering should be 1 part cement and 5 parts sharp sand, dry mixed first, then brought to a fairly stiff consistency by adding water. Before applying it to the wall, you will improve adhesion if you paint the exposed patch with a pva adhesive, such as Unibond, diluted with five parts water. While it is tacky, trowel on the first coat of rendering. Leave it to harden, but before it sets, scratch the surface with a knife or chisel to give a key for the finishing coat. This is either trowelled smooth with the wall, or if the finish is stucco, implanted with pebbles about two hours later.

All surfaces that are in good condition should be cleaned off with a stiff hand brush to remove loose particles and flaking paint.

As a wall finish, you can choose from the well-known cement paints, exterior quality emulsion, and the newer crushed stone or resin-based materials, such as Silexene and Sandtex. If the surface has been previously covered with emulsion, you may first need a sealer, and the maker's instruction should be read carefully before you go to work. For use in conjunction with Sandtex is a stabilising solution that is said to lock firmly back to the wall the dusty surface often found on smooth rendered walls. Apply the chosen finish with a part-worn or cheap new 6 in. distemper brush or paint roller, protecting pipes and adjacent woodwork from splashes, for they will be difficult to remove. When using a powder and water mix, do not make up more than you can apply in about an hour. On a stucco finish, brush the material well into the pebbles – and allow about 30 per cent more material than you would need for a smooth-rendered finish.

PROTECTING TIMBER CLADDING

Lots of modern houses have panels of natural-finished timber cladding as decorative relief on the exterior, which must be rigorously maintained if its appearance is to remain attractive. If the timber is unprotected, the elements will bleach out its natural colour and dirt will discolour it further. All it needs is a little thought and care – not unremitting devotion.

The least expensive treatment to apply is also the easiest – a water repellant combined with a colour or wood preserver to beat off wood-boring insects. Most exterior cladding is Western Red Cedar, and though this is unpalatable to insects, it turns a dull grey under the attack of sun and rain, so specialist firms such as Cuprinol Solignum and Rentokil market preservatives containing pigments that restore the colour, as well as keeping out the rain. For light-coloured timbers such as knotty pine, there are clear preservatives that keep out insects and moisture.

They give a pleasant matt sheen to the wood and show up the grain. All you have to do is wash the woodwork down with a solution of household detergent and allow it to dry before applying the preservatives to the bare wood; afterwards you can then forget about it for up to five years, depending on the exposure to salt air, sunshine and industrial pollution. The water repellancy is good for this period, but the colour agent may not be.

If you prefer a high gloss finish, apply an exterior-quality varnish. Four coats will be needed, and two of them should be applied before the cladding is erected, so that all ends and edges can be treated, as well as the visible surfaces. Properly applied, this treatment should last for up to three years without attention. The Timber Research and Development Association does not recommend the exterior use of polyurethane coatings in such situations unles they are protected by an exteriors quality varnish. The main difficulty is that these materials crack under the expansion and contraction of the wood, and once damp gets underneath, the coating begins to break down. Once you see signs of breakdown, remove all dirt and rub the area with fine glasspaper and touch up with two coats of varnish. If the elements have got at the bare wood and bleached it, the discoloration will have to be camouflaged with a matching wood stain before treatment. Badly discoloured timber should be completely stripped and treated with an all-over coat of a colour restorer such as Kingston's Colorbac. After filling nail holes, splits, etc., with a matching exterior quality stopper, you can then apply any of the appropriate preservatives mentioned.

Any of the whitewood claddings can be attractively finished with the coloured preservatives in the Cuprinol Timbergay and Solignum architectural ranges. These are basically water and insect repellants with pigments added that turn timbers turquoise, blue, gold, red and other eye-catching colours without obscuring its grain.

Chapter 10: DEALING WITH DAMP AND CONDENSATION

Moisture is probably the biggest single cause of the deterioration of decorations in the home. It causes wallpaper to stain and can break down the adhesive so the paper begins to peel away from the wall. Persistent, heavy dampness will eventually cause the plaster on the wall to disintegrate. More often than not, it is moisture that causes a paint film to break down, and woodwork left to the mercies of dampness will begin to decay.

There are several causes of dampness and it is not always easy for a layman to trace the source; indeed, there could be more than one cause. In serious cases, it's always best to call in expert help, but an intelligent grasp of the factors contributing to conditions of dampness can save you a lot of unnecessary expense, worry and wasted effort.

Dampness mostly affects walls and the three main causes of it are penetration of the brickwork by moisture from outside, damp rising from the ground due to the absence of a damp proof course in the walls – or a defective one – and condensation.

PENETRATING DAMP

Dampness caused by the absorption in the wall of driving rain is theoretically possible, but not common. If the main walls are of cavity construction – that is an inner and outer skin of brickwork 2 in. apart and tied together at frequent intervals with metal straps – the water cannot pass across the gap unless a careless bricklayer has made a bridge across parts of the cavity with mortar droppings. Many older houses will have solid brick walls, 9 or 13½ in. thick. Usually, the 9 in. wall is given the additional protection of a concrete rendering with a smooth or pebble-dash finish and breaks in this could produce localised damp patches on the inside walls after heavy rain. In a $13\frac{1}{2}$ in. wall, water will evaporate to the surface before it has had time to penetrate the full thickness.

The most likely cause of moisture penetration from the outside is the cumulative effect resulting from defective guttering, down-spouts, waste and overflow pipes in the plumbing system, and gaps around doors and windows caused by shrinkage of the frames from the brickwork and sometimes the absence of a drip channel on the underside of a window sill. So if you find intermittent damp patches appearing inside, the likely cause could be any one or more of these potential trouble spots.

Guttering should be cleared out twice a year of dust, leaves and other debris that build up to cause overflows. New brackets should be fixed to support sagging lengths, which could make a low point for water to collect and subsequently overflow. Check that downspouts are not clogged and have a clear outfall into a gulley. Over the years, a build-up of grit and corrosion within downspouts can produce severe blockages that are difficult, if not impossible, to remove. Displaced or missing roof tiles are the likely causes of damp patches on or near upstairs ceilings. So are fractured or disturbed lead flashings around chimney stacks and window bays, door porches, etc.

If there is no rendering over the brickwork, run an old knife into the mortar between the brick courses. If this is crumbling, you have another possible source of water penetration and the brickwork may need wholely or partly repointing. If the walls are rendered, inspect them carefully for cracks and bulging patches. The one will lead to the other as water infiltrates the crack, soaks the surrounding brickwork and loosens the rendering. Cracks should be filled and defective areas patched, as described in Chapter 9. Decorative treatments that are protective as well are also described in that chapter, but there is another way that over-porous brickwork can be rendered waterproof. This is to brush into the surface a silicone water repellent. There are several brands on the market, and, being colourless, they will not spoil the mellow appearance of well-weathered bricks, which can be a decorative treatment in their own right. Properly applied, silicone repellents can last for ten years or more.

However, when damp-proofing a wall, it is essential that

residual moisture should be allowed to evaporate through one side or the other. Walls should never be sealed on both surfaces, so before you decide on this treatment, read the remarks later in this chapter on the advantages of waterproofing walls from the inside.

RISING DAMP

Potentially more serious and a greater nuisance is rising damp. It will appear on ground floors to a height of up to 3 or 4 ft. above the floor, and, unlike damp patches caused by water penetration, will usually be there, even in warm dry weather. In time, it will cause the plaster to crumble and could cause decay in nearby timbers. As the name suggests, rising damp is caused by moisture in the soil being drawn up into the walls and the standard way to prevent this is to insert a damp proof course – dpc – which is an impervious sheet material in the foundations of the walls two or three courses of brickwork up from the ground level. Many old houses do not have a dpc, and in houses that do, it could be defective, due to deterioration through age, or breakage due to settlement of the walls.

A damp course can also be rendered useless by allowing flower beds to be piled above it and by paths to be laid too close to it. The ground level should be maintained 6 in. below the damp course which will usually be visible in an extra-thick band of mortar.

There are several methods of providing a damp course to an existing house. The traditional method involves inserting a layer of bitumenous felt or overlapping slates in the appropriate brick course, cutting away and rebuilding a section of the brickwork at a time, but there are new systems that are quicker to install than this and can be carried out without interference with the inside of the house. One is to 'drip-feed' through a series of holes drilled into the bricks a liquid that is soaked up by the bricks to form an impervious band. Another system, carrying a 20-year guarantee, is available from Rentokil under the impressive name of electro-osmosis. In all damp walls there is a tiny electrical charge which is what causes the damp to creep up the walls. The Rentokil system diverts this charge to earth through a rod driven deep into the ground, which is connected to a continuous copper strip embedded in the walls of the house.

None of these processes is cheap, but there are less expensive methods of dealing with rising damp. They involve covering it, rather than curing it. You can use a clear silicone water repellent, but this might merely drive the water elsewhere, to create new damp patches. So play safe and treat the whole of an affected wall. You must be sure to remove all vestiges of paper, paint, adhesive, etc., from the wall so that the plaster can soak up the repellent. At least two coats will be needed, with a 24-hour drying time between each, and very porous plaster will need three. To redecorate the wall, apply decorator's size over the repellent, then stick lining paper to the wall. This can either be painted or wallpapered. The repellent will not provide an effective key for paint.

An alternative that is quicker and generally effective is to stick aluminium cooking foil to the stripped wall with a latex rubber adhesive, such as Copydex. Overlap the joints by about ¼ in. and then apply lining paper.

Another way to tackle this problem is to create a sort of cavity wall, to keep the damp at bay and there are two ways in which you can do this. From inside the room, you could create a false wall of decorative timber cladding or plain hardboard which can be painted or papered. The gap will prevent the damp from staining the visible surface, and the techniques for applying this kind of covering are described in Chapter 5. When erecting cladding on a damp wall, an additional precaution should be taken. First apply to the bare plaster a waterproof membrane such as a silicone repellent or foil. Then treat the wall battens on all sides and edges with a wood preservative, as sold for use on exterior timbers. The whole of the affected wall should be covered.

If you clad the wall internally, there will be an additional bonus during the winter. The air space between the cladding and the actual wall will prevent a lot of the warmth produced by the source of heat from 'leaking' away through the wall. Home owners sufficiently interested to read this book will be on nodding terms with thermal insulation, but the principles are dealt with in more detail later in this chapter.

The alternative to internal wall cladding is to create a little dry moat around the affected walls, so that moisture in the earth is not absorbed by the bricks, and such moisture that is in them has a chance to evaporate outwards. Dig a trench 1 ft. wide and about 18 in. deeper than the internal floor level. Pour concrete into this trench to a thickness of about 3 in. and give it a pronounced slope from the house wall to the earth. The earth can be held back from the trench by a brick or stone wall built to ground level or well preserved timber boards nailed to posts. Obviously, the brick or stone wall will last longer, but you should get ten years or more life from a properly preserved timber construction. At the base of this retaining wall make small outlets at about 2 ft. intervals, so that water can drain from the trench into the soil. Before digging the trench, find out where gas, water and electricity supplies enter. If there is a danger that your excavations would uncover them, consult first with the appropriate authorities. Approached the right way, they are unlikely to be unsympathetic to your aims, and may be able to help you overcome the difficulties involved. The same reasoning applies where waste drains from the house get in the way, and to sort this one out you must contact the local authority building or health inspector.

CONDENSATION

If penetrating damp and rising damp are not your problems, you will be very lucky if you do not have to cope with damp produced by condensation. This can just as easily ruin decorations and cause mildew on clothes, bedding and similar perishable items when stored in unventilated cupboards. Understand the principles that cause condensation, and you are half-way towards finding a cure.

All air contains a certain amount of water vapour and the warmer the air is, the more moisture it can hold. When warm air is cooled, the water vapour it was supporting until that moment suddenly condenses into actual beads of moisture. That's precisely what happens on your windows in the winter – the air is warmed by your fire or central heating system, the warm air rises and spreads, and wherever it strikes a window or cool surface, it will shed some of its moisture as condensation.

Apart from the natural moisture content in the air, there is the moisture we add to it artificially every time we boil a kettle, wash up, run a bath – even breathe out. Portable paraffin heaters produce, as a by-product of combustion, about 1 gallon of water for every gallon of paraffin; gas heaters, unless connected to a flue, about 1½ lb. of water for every lb. of gas burnt. Electric and solid fuel heaters, and most central heating systems, do not produce moisture in this way.

Thus, we can artificially inject into the air more moisture than it can support and the result will be either a temporary attack of condensation, or the aggravation of an existing problem.

What's to be done about it? The answer lies in a careful balance of adequate ventilation and heating, but don't think solely in terms of stepping up the level of your heating, for this could prove ruinously expensive and unnecessary. What you must first aim to do is to stop the heat you are already producing from escaping through the outside walls and windows – just as blankets stop the natural warmth of your body from escaping into the cold night air; as a tea cosy keeps a pot of tea warm. The inside surfaces of outside walls must be insulated as much as possible, so that they remain at room temperature. The best form of insulation, if your house has cavity walls, is an injection of an insulant such as foamed polystyrene to fill the cavity. If you have solid walls, or cannot afford the high cost of this specialist treatment, the same effect can be partially achieved by several means from inside the house. Thin-gauge polystyrene is manufactured in rolls for sticking direct to plaster as an underlay for wallpaper. It has some effect, but being soft, it will dimple easily and permanently if knocked, and be ruined if ever the wallpaper has to be stripped. Some of the heavy-duty sheet vinyl wall coverings have a good insulation value, and so has cork. But probably the best alternative to cavity wall insulation is a wall cladding, as described earlier in this chapter as a by-pass for rising damp, and in Chapter 5 as a decorative finish in its own right. Timber is a poor conductor of heat, so therefore has some insulation value, and the barrier of still air behind makes an added insulant. If you fill this cavity with the sort of mineral wool blanket advertised for insulating the roof space, or stick polystyrene ceiling tiles directly to the wall under the cladding, or tack cooking foil to the battens before applying the cladding, you are beginning to approach the thermal efficiency of the cavity wall injection. These treatments are necessary only on the room surfaces of exterior walls.

Windows can be protected against condensation attack by applying double glazing and there are many types to choose from. At its simplest, you can make your own double glazing by purchasing rebated wooden beading from a timber yard, glass cut to size from a merchant, and making the whole lot up into frames that are screwed to the existing window frames. Kits consisting of an extruded flexible plastic strip designed to fit round a second pane of glass, and turnbuckles to hold the units in place are another inexpensive alternative. However, if you don't ensure a perfect seal between the new panes and the existing frame, a mild form of condensation, or misting between the panes, could occur, and dust would gradually build up. Both would be extremely troublesome to remove. A superior type of kit for home assembly consists of components to make rigid secondary frames, which can be fitted as sliding or hinged windows for easy cleaning and ventilation. There are also several nationally-known firms, such as Rentokil, that specialise in the installation of hinged or sliding double-glazing units to existing frames.

Once these basic exterior surfaces have been insulated, you can turn your attention, if needs be, to increasing the level of heating. But even if you possess, or are thinking of having central heating installed, insulation should be the first consideration. At its best, it will result in fuel economies that will wipe out the cost of the treatment in a few years.

The most effective way to deal with the temporary condensation that occurs during cooking, washing and bathing, is to increase ventilation. In its crudest form, this would be to open a door or window – an unfriendly act on a cold day. Much better to fit an electric extractor fan, which will swiftly remove the steamy air from bathroom or kitchen, allowing drier, warm air from the rest of the house to replace it. A new lightweight and inexpensive model is the Philips Window Fan, made from tough, transparent plastics.

It is a common practice, in the interests of preserving warmth, to block off room ventilators, usually found near the ceilings of outside walls, and to do this will, of course, aggravate the problem.

The materials used in decorating can also alleviate the nuisance of condensation, and the best choice is a hard tough surface that is easily wiped dry and will resist a steady film of moisture. Ceramic tiles will retain their sheen and fresh colour throughout many years of attack. So will the plastic laminates. The pebbly-textured heavy vinyl wall coverings are tough enough to withstand continual cleaning down and their large surface area will hold a film of condensation for longer than a smooth, glossy surface, where the moisture will soon bead and turn into rivulets. For the same reason, emulsion and flat oil paints will hold moisture as a film where it would soon start to run on a glossy enamel surface. But the glossy enamel will generally stand up longer to condensation than will matt-finished paints. There are also anti-condensation paints, formulated to hold the moisture and withstand its effects, but are more suited to the industrial applications for which they were developed than domestic settings.

Chapter 11: ODD JOBS TO DO FOR THE FINISHING TOUCHES

FIRM FIXINGS

To add the finishing touches to a decoration scheme you will inevitably become involved in such allied tasks as putting up new-style curtain tracks or pelmets, fixing wall cupboards, or merely hanging a picture over the fireplace. All these jobs and many others, depend on firm wall fixings, and the brickwork will have to be plugged so that screws can be inserted, or you will have to use masonry nails – specially hardened to drive securely into brick, stone and concrete.

Mostly, you will achieve better fixings with screws and wall-plugs. Wall-plugs used to come in a large range of sizes to suit each size of screw, but the modern ones greatly simplify the handyman's requirements. They are made from tough plastic, which will not split as the fibre ones were prone to do. One size will cover screw sizes 6, 8 and 10, which will cover most domestic needs. This also means that only one size of tungsten carbide tipped masonry drill is needed – $\frac{1}{4}$ in.

Holes should be drilled so that the full length of the plug will be in the brickwork and not partly in the surface plaster. One of the slower speeds on a variable-speed electric power tool should be chosen for drilling. As an alternative, a hand drill is better than a single speed power tool, which will quickly burn the specially hardened tip of the drill, if not used with great care. Apply moderate pressure to the drill and withdraw it from the hole frequently to allow the dust to clear. Generally the hole should be about $1\frac{5}{8}$ in. deep, which allows 1 in. penetration into brick. A strip of adhesive tape wrapped round the shank of the drill $1\frac{5}{8}$ in. from the tip will act as a depth gauge, but the final indication of whether the hole is deep enough will come when the plug is inserted. The colour of the dust will tell you what material you are drilling into. If it's red, obviously you are into brick, which could be hard or soft. If it's charcoal grey, you are probably drilling moulded building blocks, which are bored through easily and cleanly. If the colour is a light yellowish grey, you are almost certainly drilling concrete, which can be very difficult to bore. A common trouble spot is a concrete lintel over a window. If the drill seems to be making no progress, the tip has probably met a small flint in the concrete, and the friction could burn out the tip. In these circumstances, you need an old-fashioned 'jumping tool' a form of pointed chisel, to break down the flint before drilling can proceed.

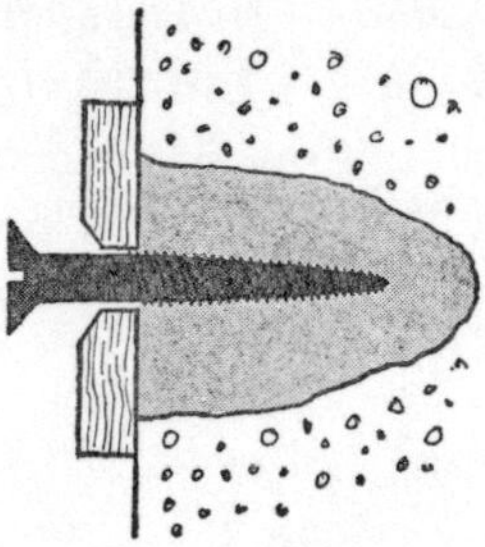

Fig. 27. Plastic filler for uneven holes in brickwork

Sometimes, soft brickwork will crumble into a hole too large for the appropriate plug. When this happens, use one of the proprietary asbestos compounds. These are sold in powdered form which becomes plastic when moistened. Roll it into a worm and ram it well into the hole with the small tool provided with each packet. Ramming will force the material to fill an uneven hole, and it will dry into a secure fixing for a screw. (See Fig. 27.) Some people prefer to use this material rather than individual plugs.

There are special devices for getting firm anchorages into cavities, such as modern flush doors, which have no hard core into which a screw will bite, and into a ceiling between the joists. Made from metal or plastic, they work by being passed through a hole into the cavity on the end of a bolt or screw. When these are tightened, the device spreads out and is drawn tight against the back of the hole. Fig. 28 shows three types from the Rawlplug range.

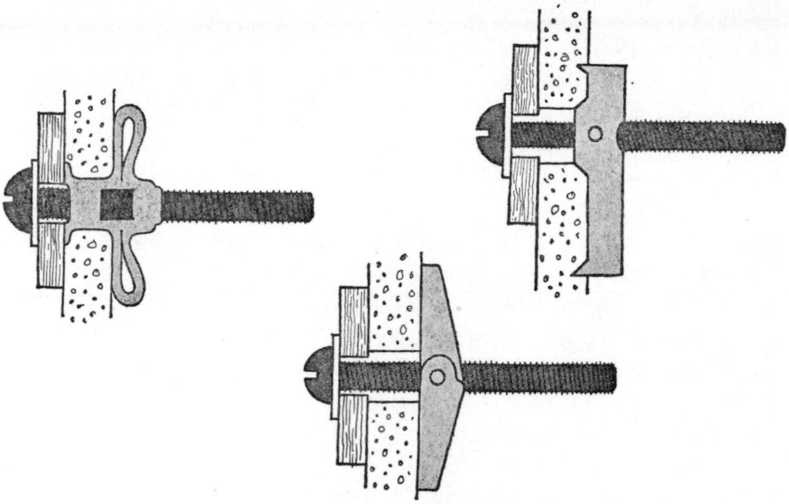

Fig. 28. Three types of Rawlplug cavity fixings

Masonry nails would be used mostly to provide a quick fixing for wall battening, but the hardening process makes them rather brittle and they must be hammered home with care or they might snap off. Make sure you strike the nail square on, and drive it in with short sharp blows a fraction at a time. The nail should penetrate beyond the plaster into $\frac{3}{4}$ to 1 in. of brickwork. For hanging pictures, there are special thin, hardened pins, each supplied with a small brass hook from which the picture cord can be suspended.

In modern houses, partition walls between rooms are sometimes hollow, consisting of two skins of plasterboard over a groundwork of timber framing. When fixing bookshelves or cupboards to such walls, it is essential to locate the timber frames and drive screws into these. It requires a laborious, trial-and-error routine of tapping the plasterboard until you detect a solid sound that tells you there is a timber frame behind. It will help in locating them if you remember that frames are generally of 3 in. sq. timber placed at 16 in. intervals vertically and 24 in. horizontally. For lightweight items on hollow walls, you could use the cavity fixing devices just mentioned.

REMOVING AN OLD FIREPLACE

The ever-growing trend to central heating and use of gas or electric fires is making more and more fireplaces redundant. Often, there is no need to do more than box in an ugly tiled surround, but if you remove it, you will find the possibilities for improvement to the room's decorative scheme will increase out of all proportion to the effort involved. It's a job that calls for brawn, rather than brain, and you might need a little help from a friend.

Begin by sweeping the chimney to remove the worst of the accumulated soot. Cleaning to professional standards isn't necessary, and you can do it yourself by dropping a large bag of stones down the flue on the end of a rope, or dragging a home-made brush of twigs through it. Seal off the fireplace end to contain the dust while working.

Chop away a small area of plaster on either side of the surround close to the mantelshelf. This will expose the metal lugs which are screwed to the wall to hold the surround in place. At a corresponding point near the base of the surround, there might be two similar lugs. Take out the screws, if they are not too corroded, and the fireplace will be ready to dismantle. If the screws won't budge, lever the fireplace away from the wall with a crowbar. The surround could be in one piece or consist of a top mounted on two uprights. Either way, it will be extremely heavy, so be careful that it doesn't come away suddenly, causing an accident, and get assistance to dump it. With the surround removed, you can prise the hearth loose in a similar way and break up the fireplace back. The void behind it will be full of rubble which should be removed, and the hole cleaned up with a stiff brush.

Rather than disturb the small inset hearth often found in bedroom fireplaces, it would be simpler to hack off the tiles and build up to floorboard level with hardboard.

If you intend to replace the old grate with a gas fire, consult the gas board as there are certain requirements regarding a connection to the flue. If an electric fire is to be fitted, the hole will have to be filled with a panel of asbestos, plywood or blockboard and access for wiring provided. Again, this is something to consult an electrical contractor about. Fixings for a panel can be made by running 2 × 1 in. battens around the opening, securing them with masonry nails or screws and wall-plugs. They should sit within the opening at a distance equal to the thickness of the panel material, so the panel sits flush with the face of the brickwork.

For a more permanent finish, brick the opening up.

Whichever method you choose, some provision for the ventilation of the flue must be made, though this will be automatic when a gas fire is installed. It is to prevent dampness within the chimney, which could eventually produce stains on the visible surface of the chimney breast. Insert a metal or plastic ventilation grille in any panel, or an airbrick if you brick the opening up. If you think that this treatment would spoil the finished appearance of the wall, you might prefer to seal off the chimney to keep it dry. Metal caps made specially to drop over the top of a chimney pot can be purchased from some builders merchants, or you could make up your own quite cheaply with two or three layers of roofing felt tied round the pot and coated with a bitumenous mastic.

REPAIRING A BROKEN WINDOW PANE

First, the cracked pane or the remnants of a shattered one must be removed, and an old burglar's trick will help to prevent flying splinters: Stick a sheet of tough brown paper to the inside of the broken pane. After hacking off the putty with an old chisel, you will find at intervals around the pane, glazier's sprigs – small headless pins used to support the glass. When these have been removed, the remnants of the pane can be lifted out clean on the paper backing.

Ideally, the rebate of a timber window frame should be given a coat of priming paint before the new pane is installed, but to do so will not always be practical and it is not a critical need. The pane is sealed in ordinary linseed oil putty, which should be of a consistency that allows it to be worked into a 'rope' of about ¾ in.-diameter that will not break when stretched over six or seven inches. If it is not sufficiently pliable, knead in a few drops of linseed oil. To order the new pane, measure carefully the overall width and length of the frame opening and subtract ⅛ in. from each dimension. These are the measurements to which your glazier should cut the new pane.

Work the putty into a pear-shaped ball and use the thumb to press it into the rebate in a thick, continuous bed. The easiest way to apply it is to the bottom rebate first, then upwards along the sides, and finally the top.

Carefully offer the new pane up and gently press it into the rebate. Apply pressure only to the corners of the pane. The surplus putty will be squeezed out around the back of the glass and can be trimmed off later. Glazier's sprigs or small panel pins should be tapped home with the heads left about $\frac{1}{8}$ in. proud of the frame, so that they support the pane. One near each corner and, on tall windows, one or two along each side, will be sufficient. To drive the pins home, press them lightly against the glass and the rebate with an index finger. The head of a lightweight hammer can then be laid against the pane which will act as a guide for driving the pin. Swing the hammer in short arcs, keeping the edge of its head always against the pane.

Apply the fronting putty in the same way as you did the bedding putty and shape it into a neatly bevelled finish, mitred at the corners, with a putty or stripping knife. The bevels should be angled so that about $\frac{1}{8}$ in. of the rebate behind the glass can still be seen. When the putty is dry, ready for painting, the paint should be brushed over the putty on to the glass for $\frac{1}{8}$ in. This is most important to produce a weatherproof seal, and if the bevels are finished as described, the paint seal will not be seen from inside the window.

Metal frames are reglazed in basically the same way, but ordinary putty is not suitable; you must ask the glazier for metal casement putty. Obviously, sprigs cannot be driven into the frame, and instead, sprung glazing clips are fitted into tiny holes drilled in the frames. If you are careful, you will be able to re-use the existing clips. A little more attention to the rebate of a metal frame might be necessary. If there is any sign of rust, glasspaper the metal to a bright finish, apply a rust inhibitor, and allow to dry before putting in the new pane.

FIXING MIRRORS

Mirrors should never be fixed flat against a wall. In the first place, a small gap is needed to allow the circulation of air, which will prevent condensation from weakening the silvering. Also, where the wall is uneven, there is a risk when tightening the screws of putting pressure across a high spot in the wall and cracking the mirror. Large mirrors with holes drilled at the corners to receive screws should be laid on strips of foamed rubber or a similar resilient material which will act as a cushion between the mirror and the wall, and fill in any hollows. Alternatively the mirror could be screwed to battens which have been screwed into wall-plugs, or held clear of the wall by washers threaded over the screws. Be careful not to over-tighten the screws against the mirror face.

Small mirrors can be fixed with metal brackets rather like photo mounts and most ironmongers stock heavier brackets for larger mirrors.

But the easiest type of fixing is that supplied with Verity mirrors, a type made and promoted by the glass industry for do-it-yourself installation, and packed complete with supporting brackets, screws and wall-plugs. The two bottom holes are drilled first and the brackets fixed. The mirror is rested on these while the positions for the top and side brackets are determined and then drilled. All but the bottom clips are adjustable, so these holes do not have to be spot on. The bottom two must be, or the mirror will not be straight. Don't rely on measuring up from the floor to align the bottom holes. Mark the point at which you want the bottom of the mirror to rest and draw a truly horizontal line with the aid of a spirit level. To cope with uneven walls, thin washers are supplied with the mirror, and these should be inserted as necessary between the clips and the wall as packing pieces. In kitchens and bathrooms, use plenty of these washers to keep the back of the mirror wall clear of the walls.

FIXING PLASTIC LAMINATE

If you have an old kitchen unit or table that's dying on its feet, a smart worktop of plastic laminate will give it a new lease of life. Laminates such as Formica and Arborite are available in a range of ready-cut sizes, and in 8 × 4 ft. sheets, but most stockists will cut a piece to any size you like. It's best to fit laminate fractionally oversize, and plane or file the overlap flush with the edges afterwards. The thin domestic grades can be cut swiftly and cleanly with a special hooked blade made to fit the Stanley trimming knife, or with a fine-tooth saw. Always saw into the decorative side of the material.

Clean the surface to be covered, removing any loose paint, dirt and grease, otherwise you won't get satisfactory adhesion. Spread a thin coat of a contact adhesive, such as Superstik or Evo-stik, over the surface to be covered and on the back of the laminate. Leave them for about 20 minutes until touch dry. Once the two surfaces are brought together, the bond is instant, so the laminate must be positioned with accuracy. That's why you should cut it oversize, to allow a little margin for error. If possible, tack a length of flat board to one end of the surface to be covered to give a starting point against which an edge of the laminate can be rested, and place two or three lengths of timber across the worktop thick enough to support the laminate clear of it. Butt one end of the laminate hard against the guide board and use firm hand pressure to bond the first foot of laminate to the worktop. Simultaneously, remove one of the supporting timber strips and fix the next section, continuing in this way until the whole sheet is bonded.

Turn a table upside down and stand a bucket of water on it for a few hours. The weight will keep the two surfaces together while the adhesive makes its full set. Similar weights will have to be stood on a fixed worktop. Afterwards, you can trim off the surplus and attend to the edges, which should be covered for neatness. There are several treatments that you could apply. Formica make Flex-Edge, a strip made in several widths that is glued on to give a professional looking finish. Thin strips of your chosen laminate could be used, or wooden moulding fitted and varnished. Another form of neat edging is a screw-on aluminium strip which has a hollow centre into which coloured plastic strip is inserted.

FLUSHING A PANELLED DOOR

Though the fashion pendulum is swinging and panelled doors are suddenly acceptable again, many people still prefer the appearance of a flush door and would wish to cover a panelled door. Hardboard can be bought for this purpose in standard door sizes. The easiest way to flush a door is to fit a hardboard panel an inch or two smaller than the door within a moulded wooden strip with a rebate that covers the panel's edges. But it does not look as well as a panel that covers the door totally.

If the original door has an inset large top panel, this should be packed out by gluing a square of plywood to it, so that the new hardboard can be pinned to it. Handles should be removed, and you will find the door much easier to work on if you take it off its hinges and lay it flat on the floor. The hardboard should be conditioned by brushing into the mesh side about ¾ pint of clean water. Leave it to soak for 48 hours before fixing. The door should be wiped over with white spirit to remove dirt and grease.

To fix the hardboard, smear the door with a woodworking adhesive such as Dufix, around the edges and other points that will be in contact with the hardboard. Line it up carefully and fix in place with ¾ in. panel pins, following the method described in Chapter 5 (Fixing Hardboard). Strip moulding can then be glued and pinned around a small panel, or the edges of a full-size panel slightly rounded with medium and fine glasspaper.

A hole for the handle shank and a keyhole, if needed, should be drilled before any second panel goes on, using the existing holes as a guide. If both sides of a door are panelled, the strips of wood around the outside of the door frame, against which the door closes, will have to be moved, because of the extra thickness. These will be nailed to the main frame and with care, can be prised away to be reset.

INDEX